FROM THE PUBLISHE

The Business of Antiques

How To Succeed in the Antiques World

Wayne Jordan
Licensed Auctioneer & Appraiser

Copyright ©2012 F+W Media, Inc.

Published by

Krause Publications, a division of F+W Media, Inc.
700 East State Street • Iola, WI 54990-0001
715-445-2214 • 888-457-2873
www.krausebooks.com

To order books or other products call toll-free 1-800-258-0929
or visit us online at www.krausebooks.com

ISBN-13: 978-1-4402-3497-2
ISBN-10: 1-4402-3497-3

Cover Design by Jim Butch
Designed by Jim Butch
Edited by Caitlin Spaulding

Printed in USA

Contents

Section 4: Practical Tips that Work

Introduction

It's been said the antiques business is the largest unregulated trade in the world, second only to the black market. It's easy to see why: There are few barriers to enter the market (most only need a computer and an Internet connection) and inventory has never been more plentiful; transactions are usually in cash and there exists no national group to speak as one voice for the market.

But it takes a certain knack to be successful at selling high design from past eras. It's easy to see when it's lacking: Antiques businesses fail at an alarming rate. The breakneck pace of technological advancements changing this business is coupled with the break-back work to move heavy furniture or set out inventory weekend after weekend at shows. As we chronicle in each issue of *Antique Trader* magazine (for the last 57 years), successful antiques sellers are a savvy, educated bunch that know their business inside and out. During the last five years, however, that business is changing faster than many can predict or manage.

Enter Wayne Jordan. Wayne and I met in the summer of 2009 to update the skills of the average American antiques dealer. We discussed their most valuable skills this business class had spent a lifetime developing … and then talked about how current changes are quickly eroding the relevance and impact of the most important skills. Few resources exist to educate the modern dealer (whose head is also swimming with facts and concepts ranging from fakes and reproductions to the difference between Art Nouveau and Art Deco) and teach them the benefit of search engine optimization, how to post a commercial on YouTube.com or how to sell Victorian furniture to a 20-something IKEA disciple.

Wayne's approachable, never condescending, and easy-to-read columns quickly became a hit among readers. Readers appreciate his practical advice, point-by-point descriptions, and his background (He's an experienced auctioneer and personal property appraiser: read, "been there, done that.").

Our readers are succeeding and staying in business and, rather than finding themselves wondering what they will do to make their business grow next year, they are surfing on the waves of change rather than drowning in it.

Most valuable of all of Wayne's most successful tools are his flexibility and energy. It rubs off on you: "Hey, if Wayne can create a Google Places ad or create better direct mail cards and build a business for the 21st century, then so can I."

And you will with this book.

Eric Bradley
Editor
Antique Trader magazine

Section 1:
Why You Need This Book

What Antiques Dealers Can Learn From Encyclopedia Britannica

In 1993, Encyclopedia Britannica had the most profitable year in the company's history. Two years later, the company was nearly bankrupt and was sold for below book value. What happened in those two years?

Most folks would say that Britannica was done in by Microsoft Encarta. In 1993, Microsoft purchased rights to the Funk & Wagnalls Encyclopedia, created an electronic version, changed the name to Encarta, and began bundling Encarta with new computers. Encarta could be purchased off-the-shelf for around $50. Britannica sold for around $1,200. Competition from Encarta killed Britannica.

Or did it?

Did the fact that Encarta was faster, more accessible and cheaper kill Britannica or was something greater at work here? My contention is that there was something greater at work: a paradigm shift. By paradigm shift, I mean a complete change in thinking or belief system that allows the creation of a new condition previously thought impossible.

Microsoft approached Britannica in the late 1980s regarding the Encarta project, but Britannica declined to become involved. Britannica felt that involvement in an electronic encyclopedia would hurt print sales. It never occurred to Britannica that Encarta could wipe out their print sales entirely. The public experienced a complete change in thinking about encyclopedias. For slightly more than the cost of a set of encyclopedias, a family could buy a computer with an encyclopedia. The world was moving away from the library and into the den. Britannica didn't see the paradigm shift in their industry.

In America today, there is a paradigm shift occurring that will completely restructure the antiques business. What are the main drivers of the new paradigm? There are two: a soon-to-be crushing overabundance of supply and universal distribution.

Let's start by examining the supply issue.

Currently, there are seven generational cohorts in America. For our purposes, a cohort can be defined as a group that wields economic power. The largest cohort is the Baby Boomers group. Currently, Boomers are acting as caregivers and executors for their parents' generation, the Builders. Builders, for the most part, did not collect antiques; consequently, Boomers inherited the household goods of their grandparents and parents. Boomers are avid collectors of everything. Having grown up on stories of the Great Depression and wartime sacrifice, Boomers as a generation take great pride in their material possessions. There are more antiques and collectibles in private collections than in all the antique stores in America.

As a result of population shift, there is a tsunami of supply on the way. In 1995, the death rate in America was about 8 per 1,000. These are the Builders being laid to rest.

Most of their antiques and collectibles went to their children, the Boomers. But, by 2016, the death rate in America is predicted to be 26 per 1,000. The death rate will triple and this time it will be the first of the Boomers being laid to rest. It is the Boomers that have been hoarding the antiques of three generations. Antiques and collectibles will be dumped on the market at an alarming rate.

In America today, there is a paradigm shift occurring that will completely restructure the antiques business.

Who will buy these antiques and collectibles and where will they buy them? The generations following the Boomers, Generations X and Y (Millennials) simply aren't as interested in antiques as their parents were. These generations have observed their parents get the rewards of hard work: houses, cars, and material wealth. Yet they have seen the costs of their parents' success in terms of broken marriages, absentee parenting, and an epidemic of stress-related illnesses. Studies have shown that Gen X and Y are more concerned with personal relationships and lifestyle than money and material goods.

For those who do collect, don't expect them to come to your store unless your store becomes a social gathering place. Gens X and Y may love the idea of an antique store but they no longer need antique stores to make a purchase. Their purchases will be made online, from the privacy of their homes. Like the Britannica model, the paradigm is moving from Main Street to one's den.

Today, in the age of super abundance and 24/7 access, no one is waiting anxiously for the next big auction or sale catalog.

In his book, *Paradigms, the Business of Discovering the Future*, author Joel Barker claims that in a paradigm shift, everyone goes back to zero.

Everyone: Great big dealers, itty-bitty dealers, auctioneers — everyone. The playing field is leveled. Opportunity abounds for those dealers that comprehend shift and go with the flow. A brand-new thought process is required.

Are you moving ahead, or falling behind?

Elements Shifting Power from Antiques Dealers

In October 1991, the strongest storm in recorded history hit off the coast of Gloucester, Maine. Created by three storms combined into one, it was dubbed "the perfect storm," and created almost apocalyptic conditions in the Atlantic Ocean. The storm was recounted in the book, *The Perfect Storm* by Sebastian Junger and the Warner Brothers film of the same name starring George Clooney.

Another perfect storm has been brewing for some time now in the antiques business. The results of the storm, though not apocalyptic, will manifest a shift in power from the antiques dealer to the consumer, which will redefine the way business is transacted. The days of the unchallenged expertise of the dealer are over. The three elements driving the storm of change are the proliferation of social networking, mobile Internet devices, and product/pricing transparency.

The First Storm: Online Social Networking

The human desire to connect with other people has driven online social networking to triple-digit growth. As of April 2010, Facebook had more than 400 million users, and adds hundreds of thousands of new users daily. Four hundred million Facebook users are about 30 percent more than the population of the entire United States.

Add in the numbers from Twitter, MySpace, and other platforms and the number of people actively engaged in online social networking is staggering. People are connected, and they talk to each other, offer advice, and share knowledge.

The Second Storm: Mobile Devices

In 2009, there were more than 450 million mobile Internet users worldwide, according to IDC global intelligence. This number is expected to surpass the 1 billion mark by 2013. Mobile Internet will replace, and be as common as, cell phones. Internet-connected mobile devices are already reshaping the way we go about our personal and professional lives. Mobile device users regularly use search engines, read news, download podcasts, music, videos, and exchange emails.

The Third Storm: Product/Pricing Transparency

In his book, *The World Is Flat*, author Thomas Friedman asserts that one effect of global interconnectivity is the breaking down of barriers. Information on any topic is available anytime, anywhere, to anyone. Up until now, antiques dealers could be confident that the majority of their customers knew less than they did about their inventory. That is no longer the case; the information readily available via mobile Internet devices has broken down the knowledge barrier between dealer and consumer. Consumers can quickly access item descriptions, points of connoisseurship, and pricing information at websites like collect.com, kovels.com, and WorthPoint.com.

> A perfect storm has been brewing for some time now in the antiques business. The storm manifests a shift in power from the antiques dealer to the consumer, redefining the way business is transacted.

On the leading edge of the antiques information revolution is Will Seippel, a lifelong collectibles dealer, executive, college professor, and creator and CEO of WorthPoint.com.

Seippel combined his experience creating databases for the airline and telecom industries with his knowledge of collectibles to create the WorthPoint database.

According to Seippel, WorthPoint aggregates pricing information from the top 50 auction houses, including eBay market data, TIAS, and sister site GoAntiques.com. WorthPoint also offers access to research articles and certified appraisers, designated "Worthologists." Of course, mobile devices are supported.

Although many dealers and appraisers subscribe to the database, consumers are WorthPoint's targeted market. According to Quantcast.

com, 81 percent of WorthPoint's visitors are non-antiques professionals in the 35-and-up age and $100,000-plus income demographics. The service is priced for non-professionals, costing less per day than a trip to Starbucks. Clearly, the service is driven by consumer needs rather than business needs.

WorthPoint's rapid growth is proof that there is a desire for antique product and antique pricing information. Since beginning in April 2009 as a subscription site, WorthPoint has enrolled over 20,000 paid subscribers, and has over 100,000 users per day, including free trial users. Quantcast ranked them as number 758 for site traffic in the United States, with more than 10 times the traffic of their closest competitor after only 18 months of operation. WorthPoint is growing at over 5 percent per month, in an economy where 2 percent growth per year is considered impressive. Seippel estimated that WorthPoint had over 10,000 paid subscribers by the end of 2010, and growth was expected to continue to skyrocket with their recent product release.

In the fall of 2010, WorthPoint rolled out a new product, a database, which completed the "perfect storm" scenario.

Before its release, Seippel predicted that the new database would add over 10 million records per month, and have the capability to store over 1 billion records and 10 billion photos. Think about it: 10 billion. Look up into the sky on a clear night, and you will see roughly 10 billion stars.

In addition, WorthPoint is digitizing antique periodicals and textbooks. Their research taxonomy will go four levels deep, ending with a wiki that will drive the information database even deeper.

At-will access to such an antiques and collectibles database gives a clear advantage to consumers.

No longer will a consumer settle for pennies on the dollar when selling items to a dealer. With up-to-date information, private sellers can list their items online, give accurate descriptions, set competitive prices or reserves without guessing, and make more money than they could when selling to a dealer. When buying, a consumer can cross-check a dealer's price to see if they are fair, and quickly access the information they need to determine if the item they are contemplating is authentic.

Of course, there have always been consumers savvy enough to compete with the experience of a dealer. It is commonplace to see bidders attend an auction carrying a printed collectibles guide. In the perfect storm scenario, however, anyone with mobile Internet access and decent search skills can compete effectively, regardless of their age or experience.

What does this perfect storm mean for antiques dealers? Antiques dealers and auctioneers are already reporting a higher number of shoppers armed with mobile devices.

Within the next four years, it is anticipated that Internet-ready mobile devices will have replaced cell phones. At that point, virtually everyone attending an auction or shopping in a showroom will be equipped to refer to online pricing and product information.

Dealers suggest that mobile devices will likely not affect sales to in-store browsers or impulse purchasers.

High-end sales and sales to collectors will be impacted.

As prices go up, buyers are more cautious. High-end sales will still be made, but profit margins will suffer. Antiques dealers who are unwilling to negotiate their markups will find their inventory turns will slow down, and over all profitability will suffer as a result. Dealers can also expect to pay more for their purchases.

Dealers will need to be aware of what is being said online about items they have in their inventory.

Where a relationship of trust has not been established between the buyer and seller, information a buyer gleans from an "authority" website, right or wrong, will carry more weight than a dealer's opinion. The dealer needs to sharpen his sales skills to sway a buyer toward his item.

The way for an antique dealer to survive the coming perfect storm is be as tech-savvy as his customers, and stay current with both the available technology and the developing information products.

Inventory, Investment, and Perception

How can you move merchandise when there's blood in the streets?

Baron von Rothschild, the 19th-century British banking magnate, had a succinct investment philosophy: "The time to buy is when there is blood in the streets, even if that blood is your own." The Baron would know: He made a fortune in the panic that followed Napoleon's defeat at the battle of Waterloo.

Modern-day billionaires echo the Baron's philosophy. Warren Buffett and other "contrarian" investors scoop up deeply discounted corporate assets whenever markets turn down. In Buffet's own words: "You pay a very high price in the stock market for a cheery consensus."

Of course, in a depressed market, cash is king. It's likely that von Rothschild and Buffett had money to invest. Even teenage entrepreneurs know the adage, "It takes money to make money." Cash-strapped antiques dealers are aware of the "good deals" to be had in the current market, but many don't have the cash or the credit to pursue the available opportunities. How, then, can an antiques dealer raise the cash to take advantage of current depressed prices? The Baron had the answer in 1815: Shed some blood.

The difference between success and failure is that some are willing to see blood in the streets, even if it is their own.

As I traveled and shopped at antiques markets and shows last summer, I had the opportunity to speak with dealers and watch them ply their trade. I found four attitudes to be prevalent among the dealers at the shows I attended. The first concerns the overall business atmosphere, but the other three attitudes I found mostly among the dealers who complained that business was bad and they weren't making any money. Here's what I found:

1. There is a lot of business being done, despite the "troubled times." Dealers were excited about the prices they were paying for fresh inventory. Consumers were still buying antiques and collectibles. Shows were attracting record numbers of attendees, and money was changing hands.

2. Many dealers were reluctant to sell any inventory at a loss. More than once, I observed a dealer walk away from a deal declaring, "I can't sell that for less than I paid for it." Dealers who persist in that philosophy may eventually find themselves facing a bankruptcy judge. In any free market, prices and values go up and down. Would these dealers expect the value of their stock portfolio to never go down? How about the value of their home?

The very definition of "market value" is what a willing buyer pays a willing seller, neither being under duress. Dealers, your inventory may be worth less than you think. What you paid for an item has absolutely nothing to do with what its market value is when the time comes to sell it.

Holding on to over priced inventory slows your inventory turns, ties up your cash and increases your taxes. Either sell slow-moving items at a discount, or write down the cost basis of the inventory. Doing so will increase your cost-of-goods-sold and lower your gross profit, but it will also decrease your tax bill. In a down economy, do you really want to be paying more taxes?

When you sell the slow-moving inventory at a discount, you free up cash to buy new inventory that can turn over faster and increase your profitability. Yes, it's sometimes difficult to take a loss on an item, but as von Rothschild said, sometimes the blood in the streets must be your own.

3. Some dealers were inclined to look at their inventory as a collection of individual items instead of an organic whole.

Inventory is an investment, much like a stock portfolio. Within the portfolio, individual stocks will rise and fall in value. At the end of the year, it is the performance of the portfolio as a whole that makes money or loses money. During the course of the year, individual stocks are evaluated as to their performance: Are they bringing a return on investment or not?

If they are not, then they are sold at a loss, and new investments are made. Antiques dealers must consider their inventory in the same way they would consider a stock portfolio: Is an individual item bringing a return on the investment, or is the item sitting on the floor attracting dust and tying up money?

Nonperforming assets (slow-moving inventory items) should be replaced with assets that will bring a return on investment. At the end of the year, the performance of the inventory as a whole is a major factor in profitability. Consider the most common method of accounting for inventory from the IRS Schedule C.

At tax time, the cost of goods sold comes down to starting inventory plus purchases minus ending inventory. Dealers would do well to perceive their inventory the same way the IRS does: as an organic whole.

4. Few dealers understand the relationship between inventory turnover and profitability. Many antique dealers entered the business because it was a passionate hobby, but they know little about retailing. They know that if they pay X for an item and sell it for less than X that they are losing money. When inventory is considered as an organic whole and as an investment, dealers learn that quickly turning inventory increases their return on investment.

For those who are new to the concept of inventory turnover, let's review what inventory turnover is and how it impacts profitability. Inventory turnover reflects how often your inventory is sold and repurchased (turned over) within an accounting period. The formula is Inventory Turnover = Cost of Goods Sold / Average Dollar Value of Inventory On-hand. Turning inventory fast is good for cash flow and profits.

Here is an example: Let's say your cost of goods sold for the year is $100,000 on sales of $200,000. The average value of your inventory is $50,000. $100,000/50,000 = 2. You turned your inventory twice for the year and made a gross profit of $50,000 on your $50,000 investment.

Not bad.

Now, let's say that you are holding on to some slow-moving inventory, and the average value of your inventory goes up to $75,000. So let's figure the inventory turnover: $100,000/$75,000 = 1.3. You turned your inventory 1.3 times and made only $25,000 on your inventory investment. You made half as much money at the same sales level because your inventory was not turning as fast.

Dealers who do well are those who sell their inventory for what the market would bear (even at a loss) and then refresh their inventory while buying at low prices. Dealers who do poorly were those who hold on to overvalued inventory and have no money to reinvest. The difference between success and failure is that some dealers are willing to see blood in the streets, even if it was their own.

In the next chapter, let's look at the reasons why some dealers hang onto merchandise to the extent of threatening an entire business model.

Why Don't Antiques Dealers Just Cut Prices and Move Old Merch? Because We Don't Like Losing Something Once We Own It

I like having money to spend. I try not to spend it, but just having money and knowing that I could spend it if I wanted to feels good to me. I don't think that I'm alone in feeling this way, either. Money affects people in physical ways, and I recently stumbled onto proof that this is true.

In 2009, Kathleen Vohs of the University of Minnesota conducted an experiment disguised as a "dexterity study." In the study, she had one group of students count a stack of $100 bills while another group counted a similar-sized stack of blank pieces of paper. Then, both groups of students stuck their fingers into very hot water. The students who counted the real money reported feeling significantly less pain from the hot water than the students who didn't handle the money.

The effect was so pronounced that Vohs tried the experiment in reverse: She asked some subjects to make of list of their monthly expenses and another group to write about the weather. The group who listed their bills felt more pain from the hot water than the group that wrote about the weather.

Cash is so compelling as a means of exchange that antiques dealers keep plenty of it in their pockets when they go on buying trips. I've never conducted an estate sale where a dealer said to me, "I'll write you a check;" they always pull a wad of bills out of their pocket and unfold them slowly so that I get a good look at them. And you know what? The technique works. The cash looks good to me and all of a sudden I'm willing to make a deal. Most of my other estate sale customers pay by check or by plastic.

Here's an interesting corollary: Dealers may leverage their purchasing power with cash, but many of the same dealers will sit on their inventory purchases forever rather than trade them for more cash. Why is that?

Last month, I attended a festival in Southwestern Virginia and while I was there I stopped by a favorite antiques store. It was almost like going home. The larger pieces of furniture were in the same spot they were in on my last visit. In fact, even some of the smaller inventory items were in the same spot they had been in for the five years that I've lived in this area. Most museums change their displays more often than this store.

Since I'm on friendly terms with the owner, I teased him about a vintage secretary that held a display of dolls. "Are you selling your fixtures?" I asked.

"No. Why?"

With a big grin, I said, "Because there's a price tag on this secretary. It's been here so long I thought it was a fixture." (You can say almost anything if you grin real big.)

I think I embarrassed him. The excuses (uh, I mean "reasons") that the secretary was still unsold came pouring forth: "I have too much into it;" "I'm not just going to give it away;" and "I'd rather keep it than sell it cheap," all seemed to run together into one big sentence. I acquiesced and the conversation moved on to the town festivities.

Maybe on one level we are not just antiques dealers; we are psychologists with an interest in antiques.

The truth is, holding on to inventory too long is very common in the antiques trade. Even when faced with compelling financial data (like inventory turns and profits), dealers still hold on to their beloved inventory. I've never understood it until recently.

Interesting reading for any business owner is a book titled *Priceless: The Myth of Fair Value and How To Take Advantage Of It* by William Poundstone. Buried among the discussions of behavioral decision theory and research on pricing strategies, I found that there is a psychological basis for antiques dealers wanting to hang on to their inventory: It's called loss aversion. This particular loss aversion has nothing to do with losing money on an item; it's a psychological driver.

I've heard of loss aversion, but I've never before considered its impact on retail pricing. The essence of loss aversion is that simply owning something increases its value (to us). We don't like losing something once we own it. Antiques dealers are also collectors, and they tend to get attached to the items the buy.

To demonstrate, Poundstone described a classroom experiment that is regularly conducted by Eric Johnson of the Columbia University School of Business. The class is divided into two groups. The first group is shown a coffee mug, and asked how much they would be willing to pay for it. Most of the time the answer is around $4. The individual members of the second group are each given a coffee mug that is identical to the first mug, and then asked how much they would be willing to sell it for. The members of the "selling" group generally want, on average, about $8 each for their mugs.

Do humans have a built-in markup calculator? There is a considerable difference between how much we are willing to pay and how much we would be willing to sell the same item for.

Do humans have a built-in markup calculator? Not likely, but it's interesting that the experiment always shows the same result: that there is a considerable difference between how much we are willing to pay for an item and how much we would be willing to sell it for once we own it. Auctioneers and estate buyers deal with this issue regularly. How much money one paid for an item has nothing to do with how much it will sell for.

This discrepancy is called the "endowment effect," and the theory states that people place a higher value on objects they own relative to objects they do not own. One of the reasons I like to watch *American Pickers* is to watch collectors with barns full of junk (er, "collectibles") agonize over parting with just a few items, even when offered a fistful of cash. Reading *Priceless* has led me to the conclusion that maybe on one level we are not just antiques dealers; we are psychologists with an interest in antiques.

Survey Says: Small Antiques Shops Must Adopt More Strategies

I read with great interest WorthPoint's 2011 Antiques & Collectibles Survey Results, released on Feb. 14, 2011. WorthPoint is a leading provider of valuation and associated services for art, antiques, and collectibles. The survey was taken from mid-January through early February 2011, and reflects the opinions of dealers and collectors who visited the WorthPoint website during that period.

As I reviewed its survey, my initial reaction was that its results must heavily favor Internet dealers; after all, it was an online survey. As it turns out, this initial assumption about the respondents to the WorthPoint survey was incorrect. Its survey sample was not dominated by Internet-only dealers, but included dealers who used a variety of channels for buying and selling, including the Internet, trade shows, estate sales, auctions, storefronts, and traditional media.

Reading the survey results, I recalled my experience last summer when I traveled to shows and antiques stores and interviewed dealers about "the state of the business." I thought it might be enlightening to juxtapose my personal results (see *Antique Trader*'s Oct. 19, 2010, coverage of the Hillsville Market) with the results of the WorthPoint survey and attempt to assemble a balanced view of the buying and selling channels that are actually working for dealers. The WorthPoint group of respondents and my respondents were similar in makeup, so I would be comparing apples to apples in my analysis.

Just three years ago, the now-defunct Antiques Dealers TV reported that, "only 12 percent of the antique dealers polled had any Internet marketing strategy other than an eBay account." According to the 2011 WorthPoint survey, antiques dealers have since made remarkable progress incorporating the Internet into their business model. Eighty-one percent of dealers surveyed stated that the Internet was their main source of buying and selling opportunities. Sixty-one percent of WorthPoint's respondents said that the Internet was their most effective promotional tool. In contrast, only 33 percent (eight out of 24) of the dealers interviewed at the Hillsville Market even had a website. But, those eight Hillsville dealers with websites also successfully pursued sales on eBay and other online venues.

As with other retail businesses, the antiques business is being transformed by the Internet. However, it's difficult to build a sustainable Internet-only antiques business. Antiques and collectibles, by their very nature, are rare. It's difficult for a dealer to mount a killer Internet marketing plan when he's selling one-of-a-kind items, one at a time. Unlike other retailers, antiques dealers can't pick up the phone, call their wholesaler, and order a hundred more of a hot-selling item. Once an item is sold, a dealer may not be able to replace it. This makes assembling a saleable inventory a full-time job. Dealers often spend more time acquiring items than they do selling them.

For the best chance of antiques business success, multiple sale channels must be considered.

The key to analyzing the effectiveness of the Internet vs. traditional marketing channels is to separate fact from fiction and keep a broad view. Many doom and gloom articles have been written in the past few years, warning dealers that they would surely go out of business if they did not embrace the Internet.

Although there has certainly been a weaning-out of dealers in the past few years, it has not been because those dealers failed to embrace the Internet. On the contrary, there are many dealers who employ only traditional marketing methods and do quite well, and some Internet-only dealers who suffer.

Consequently, the Internet can be part of a marketing plan, but not the entire marketing plan.

What both surveys showed was that the most successful dealers do not rely on a single strategy to market their products. Consistently, one-channel-only dealers were struggling, regardless of whether the channel was traditional or online. Storefronts, show-only dealers, and auction houses who sold online were all out-performing their counterparts who had no online strategy. Interestingly, multi-channel dealers also out-performed online-only dealers. In reporting their most effective selling and/or buying channel, 40 percent

of WorthPoint respondents claimed eBay, 23 percent claimed tradeshows, 5 percent claimed auction galleries, and 23 percent claimed "other." The most effective promotional tools were reported as the Internet (61 percent), trade shows (7 percent), word of mouth (21 percent), classified ads (8 percent), and 4 percent was relegated to "other."

At the Hillsville Market, I interviewed two dozen dealers. Of the 24, 11 dealers actively sold on eBay. That's 45 percent of the total, a number that corresponds to the WorthPoint survey number regarding eBay. eBay seems to be a strong source of sales and/or inventory for the dealers who use it.

A dealer's Internet success seemed to have more to do with their inventory than their online marketing prowess. Both survey groups expressed the intent to reduce the size of their inventories and stock fewer, but higher quality, items. Inventories consisting of smaller shippable items were important to both groups.

The Hillsville dealers who were successfully pursuing Internet sales had re-configured their inventories to stock small, shippable items. Small goods sold briskly at Hillsville; decorative items, glassware, memorabilia, and musical instruments among others. Dealers did not eschew large items altogether, though; such items were sold in their stores.

The WorthPoint respondents, as well, stated that one of their key priorities for 2011 was to prune their inventories and focus on fewer items. Common WorthPoint themes were pruning collections/focusing on fewer higher-quality items, learning more about their items, gaining greater awareness/recognition for their collections, and attracting a younger demographic into the collecting passion.

Overall, dealers were split over whether the economy will have an effect on their business in 2011; 51 percent of respondents felt that their business would increase in 2011; 15 percent felt that business would decrease; and 35 percent felt that it would remain the same. Generally, the multi-resourced dealers were more positive about their businesses.

Surveys like WorthPoint's can be of great value to antiques dealers. In the absence of a strong national dealer association, there is a distinct lack of data that dealers can use as a baseline to evaluate the performance of their business. My hat's off to Will Seippel and his crew at WorthPoint. I look forward to the next survey.

Small Business Advice Gathered Over 90 Years Helps Antiques Dealers

W hat's the best advice you ever received that you failed to take? I recently considered that question, and my thoughts went down a rabbit hole that became so deep, so fast, that I expected to bump into Alice and the White Rabbit.

Yes, I should have bought Apple stock in 1986. Yes, I should have taken a raincoat to Woodstock. No, I never should have opened that second store. Although I'm not particularly good at taking advice, my hindsight is 20/20.

Humans often claim that a characteristic that sets us apart from other species is our ability to learn from one another. I've never entirely believed that. I believe that taking advice is just not natural. Right or wrong, we tend to take our own counsel. Advice is sought for comparison purposes, listened to politely and usually dismissed. Unsolicited advice is simply ignored.

Which, as often as not, gets us into trouble. As George Santayana said: "Those who cannot remember the past are condemned to repeat it." For antiques retailers, the problem is compounded by the lack of historic information about antiques retailing. We can't remember what we never learned in the first place. Most available retailing information is boilerplate about accounting and management practices, which provides little help in running our businesses day to day. Consequently, we have nowhere to turn for help except the advice of friends, colleagues, and online forums. Ouch.

Until now.

I recently had a nice chat with Chip Averwater, author of *Retail Truths: The Unconventional Wisdom of Retailing*. Chip is a third-generation retailer and owner of Amro Music in Memphis, Tenn. Amro was started by Chip's grandfather and has been operating for about 90 years. Chip says that when he was growing up, he thought "going to work" meant "tending shop," because every adult that he knew was in retail.

Ninety years of family retailing brings a lot of experience to the table, and with it, a lot of wisdom. About 12 years ago, Chip started to write down what he considered to be the "truths" of retailing. A retail "truth" is something that can only be discovered through experience. You can't learn these truths in business school. Learning these requires enrollment in the school of hands-on retailing.

Having been both a music store owner and antique shop owner, I can tell you that most of what Averwater says about musical instrument retailing applies just as well to antiques retailing — and retailing in general, actually. The book lists 427 truths about retailing. Averwater says that there are many more "truths," but his publisher wanted to keep the book under 400 pages.

Let me share with you 10 of my favorite "truths," and let's see how they might help you improve your antiques business. I will precede each "truth" with its numbered location in the book:

(1) "It looks so easy to be so hard." Isn't that the truth? What could be easier than buying low and selling high? But add in leases, insurance, inventory, advertising, payroll, employees … well, you get the picture. No wonder the failure rate for retail business startups is so high.

(385) "A little success creates a lot of overhead," and its corollary (427) "If at first you do succeed, try not to think you're infallible." Opening your first antiques store requires that you dream big and work hard. When cash flow is good, it's natural to think that we have struck gold and our first impulse is to duplicate our effort with a second location. Don't do it. Get better right where you are.

Ninety years of family retailing brings a lot of experience to the table, and with it a lot of wisdom.

(105) "Love your products, but only for their sales." One of my early auctioneering mentors once told me that I could either be an auctioneer or a collector, but not both. If it's in your inventory, sell it. You're not a museum; you're a retail store.

(41) "Holding on to inventory mistakes only makes them more costly."

We've all made bad purchases. Why make them worse by giving them shelf space, insuring them, tracking them and carrying them to shows while you wait for a buyer to duplicate your mistake?

(110) "Outside storage is an addiction." You can't sell inventory that can't be seen. Don't hide it away in your "warehouse."

(338) "You can go broke making a profit." Dealers regularly tell me that they are re-investing their profits in inventory. Good idea — to a point. Their financials look good because they show healthy profits. But profit doesn't pay bills; cash does. The IRS won't take your Philadelphia Highboy as payment for your taxes; you'll have to sell it first. You can be very profitable and still have no cash. Watch your cash!

(86) "You're not in business if you're not in show business," and its corollary, (89) "Nothing is beautiful in the wrong light." Antiques stores can be dreary places. Don't rely on your store's overhead fluorescent lights to show off your merchandise. You'd be surprised how good lighting can increase sales.

And my personal favorite:

(416) "You can't hunt two rabbits with one dog." It's easy to get sidetracked into add-on products that aren't really your area of expertise. If you're an antiques dealer, don't try to be an art prints dealer at the same time (unless you know something about art prints). Don't split your time, energy, and money; focus on your core business.

Averwater offered some parting advice on how antiques dealers can cope with a declining market: watch expenses. As our businesses grow, we tend to make commitments to employees, landlords, suppliers, and others. When sales drop off, don't be afraid to prune expenses. Trees and vines require regular pruning in order to stay healthy, and so does your business. It's possible, Averwater says, to make a healthy profit on fewer sales. "After all, they did it (made a profit) on the way up."

Section 2:
How to Sell and Protect You Bottom Line

Why the Time is Right to Open an Antiques Business

I t's my opinion that the antiques business is the only retail business worth pursuing at the moment.

Consider the problems faced by commodity consumer goods retailers: In the past decade, "Big Box" stores have put scores of Main Street retailers out of business.

Competition from online dealers has shaved commodity retail store margins so close that it can take months for a business to recover from a downturn in sales or an uptick in expenses. An army of consumers armed with smartphones can instantly compare prices on virtually every commodity offered for sale and then harangue a retailer for a matching price. When a consumer has secured the lowest price, he or she can then scan the product's QR code for additional bargains and manufacturer's coupons. In commodity retailing, margins are tight; there's not much room for error.

Not so with antiques retailers. Despite all the gloomy predictions for the antiques trade, this is the place to be. There will never be competition from "Big Box" retailers of antiques, because there will never be any.

Even the mega antiques malls are populated by "mom and pop" dealers who rent space and benefit from the mall's foot traffic. Antiques dealers have considerably more control over their product costs and selling prices than commodity retailers do.

So, profit margins on antiques are significantly better than on most consumer goods. When commodity retailers buy, they can only "buy low" if they buy in quantities. Small Main Street commodity retailers are automatically at a competitive disadvantage compared to Big Box and chain stores.

Antiques dealers buy items one-at-a-time. Even when dealers buy entire estates, they are buying a quantity of individual items rather than dozens (or hundreds) of the same item. Antiques and collectibles dealers pay what they want to pay for products, or they don't buy them. For an antiques picker, there's always another deal around the corner.

What about online competition from other antiques and collectibles dealers? Online competition in the antiques trade is nowhere near as intense as it is in commodity retailing.

In commodity retailing, selling online is all about price. A particular make and model of washing machine will be the same no matter where you buy it; only the price will vary. Not so with antiques, collectibles, or art: The condition of each item will vary, so their prices will vary.

Objects must be considered on their own merit: Is it in original condition, in the box, does it need to be cleaned, is there damage? Online product descriptions are where antiques dealers really have a chance to shine. Tell a story, make the item come alive, and make a consumer want to own the item being offered for sale. Have you seen the product descriptions for online sellers of commodities? Those descriptions couldn't sell life to a dying man.

What impact have smartphones had on antiques retailing? There's been a lot of talk in the trade about consumers checking prices with smartphones, but retail dealers tell me that they haven't seen a lot of "smartphone checking" in actual practice. From what I've heard, smartphone use is more common at auctions (and I suspect that most of the "smartphoners" are dealers). The smartphone issue has generated some lively discussion lately in online antiques forums. Smartphones are used to check historic auction sales prices of art and antiques. Some dealers — especially those who sell art — claim that the practice of posting auction results for art sales is ruining the secondary art market. You know what I say to that? Phooey!

Despite all the gloomy predictions for the antiques trade, this is the place to be in retail.

What difference does it make if a consumer knows how much a dealer paid for a painting? Why does the dealer owe the customer an apology for his markup? How much a dealer paid for an item is the cost of the merchandise, not the cost of the sale. The cost of the sale includes rent, salaries, advertising, transportation, cleaning, re-framing, repairing, and all the time and gas the dealer spent while out picking inventory. One consumer doesn't constitute the "market" for a particular item. The type of customer who would use "dealers cost" as a negotiating point is not a customer that dealers need.

There will be other consumers interested in the item; the key is to find them. Advertise. Blog about it. There are free and low-cost ways to advertise online: Use them. More interest in an item translates to a higher price, regardless of what the dealer's cost was for the item. Dealers should not be intimidated by customers' use of smartphones; instead, they should be checking the auction sales results to stay a step ahead of their customers.

Some dealers claim that the biggest threat to antiques retailing is auctions themselves (as opposed to the posting of auction results). The auction "boogeyman" doesn't exist, either. Are consumers able to buy antiques and collectibles for less at an auction? Yes, sometimes they do; but sometimes they pay a lot more.

Consumers will almost always out-bid dealers at auctions. That's why auctions shouldn't be a dealer's sole buying strategy. But dealers can still buy right at auctions. Auctioneers frequently buy at each other's auctions and re-sell their purchases at their own auctions. If auctioneers can turn a profit buying at auction and selling at auction, then certainly dealers can turn a profit buying at auction and selling at retail.

If you're an antiques dealer (or are dreaming about being one), then congratulations: You're in the right business. Become an expert in your products; know more than your customers (including how to use a smartphone). Learn to sell, one-on-one and in print. Learn to take good photos. Your website is as important as your bricks-and-mortar store, so don't neglect it.

Most of all, understand that your products are different. You're not selling commodities but unique items that can't be purchased just anywhere. You're selling history, nostalgia, and fantasy. You can engage the imaginations of your customers in a way that no other retailers possibly can. It's an exciting business to be in.

Why Are Estate Sale Businesses Booming When Antiques Shops Struggle to Pay Rent?

In almost every market, the number of traditional antiques stores continues to dwindle, while other marketing channels — estate sale companies, auction companies, consignment stores, and online venues — continue to grow.

Why?

One reason is that traditional antiques stores are expensive to operate and entail considerably more financial risk than alternative marketing channels. Another reason is that traditional antiques stores are less responsive to the social needs of the marketplace than competing companies.

These two business cornerstones — financial risk and social necessity — should compel antiques dealers to regularly re-evaluate their business model to determine if their financial risk/rewards are in balance and if their business is responsive to the social needs of their market. Profits are paramount. They pay the bills and drive growth. But, profits aren't possible without sales, and dealers who move beyond being "just another retailer" and embrace the social needs of the marketplace will discover that their phone rings off the hook and they make more sales than ever.

You see, society is currently feeling the pain of a huge demographic shift. In 1995, the death rate in America was about eight per 1,000. By 2016, the death rate in America is predicted to be 26 per 1,000. Antiques, collectibles, and secondhand consumer goods will be dumped on the market at an alarming rate. Estate executors and administrators will have their hands full disposing of all that estate property. As Ruth Stafford Peale (wife of the Reverend Norman Vincent Peale) said, the key to success in any enterprise is to "find a need and fill it." Dealers who can solve the estate property problem for executors fill a growing social need, and those dealers will prosper.

There is a tsunami of estate business on the way, but few antiques dealers are directly involved in estate liquidation. Most dealers prefer to shop estate sales for inventory rather than become involved in the hassles of liquidating an entire estate. Dealers will soon find (if they haven't already) that the abundance of estate property on the market has driven their prices so low that it is impossible to make a profit. When that gets to be the case, I say if you can't beat 'em, join 'em.

Successful dealers aren't stuck in the "I own an antiques store" mindset; they employ multiple marketing channels to move their goods, and the most promising channel today is the estate sale business. The fastest growing resale business in America is the estate sale (a.k.a. "tag sale") company, and for good reason: such businesses have low financial risk and fill the growing social need for estate liquidation.

Dealers who move beyond being "just another retailer" will discover that their phone rings off the hook and they make more sales than ever.

Ann Roberts, marketing director of the Georgia Estate Sale Network in Atlanta, has witnessed the growth of estate sale companies in her area.

"Atlanta has seen lots of foreclosures and downsizing. More and more executors are turning to estate sale companies," she said, "because they get the job done."

Antiques dealers and auction houses don't want to deal with run-of-the-mill consumer goods. Instead, they want to "cherry-pick" the best items from an estate and leave the rest behind. That leaves executors in a tough spot when they have to empty a house full of property.

Ann believes that it's the glut of certain types of estate property — Victorian furniture, crystal, china, and silver-plate in particular — that has driven the growth of estate sale companies in Atlanta.

"Antique dealers aren't buying them anymore, and sellers are afraid of the low prices they might receive at auction," she says.

So, sellers and estate executors turn to estate sale companies.

"With an estate sale, the seller has more control over the pricing," she said.

Who buys the china and silver? According to Ann, it's "older people who are missing pieces from their set, or collectors who want to compete a set."

Some consumers prefer the laid-back atmosphere of an estate sale to the fast pace of an auction. Although you'll find dealers at estate sales as well as auctions, in general estate sales attract a different crowd than an auction. More consumers are comfortable with the wheeling-and-dealing of estate sales and garage sales (negotiating from a high price to a low price) than are comfortable with the auction format (competitive bidding from a low price to a higher price). At the end of the day, estate sale companies are able to sell virtually all the estate property and hand the executor an envelope full of cash.

Auctioneers make the argument that auctions bring better prices for some types of merchandise. That's true. A good crowd of collectors bidding against each other for popular collectibles will certainly drive up prices on some items. Some, but not all. On average, gross dollars from a typical estate sale will equal gross dollars from auctioning a similar estate. Although estate sales don't have the fast-moving action of an auction, they do have the element of "time-pressure" that makes auctions successful.

When an estate sale is over, it's over. Unlike an antiques store, where most inventory items tend to linger from week to week, buyers realize that if they don't buy an item now, they won't get a second chance.

It's easy to see why estate sale companies are becoming a popular business model for antiques and collectibles dealers. Estate sale companies don't require expensive retail leases; sales are held on the estate premises. Most such companies have no lease expense at all, since the business can be operated as a home-based business. Companies that lease warehouse space for equipment and signage can do so inexpensively and month-to-month at a self-storage facility. Estate sale companies don't invest in inventory, either; they sell what's on the premises. There is no inventory risk associated with estate sales; since there is no cost of goods, every item sold generates a gross profit for the estate sale company. Plus, selling an executor on the idea of an estate sale is relatively easy. The combination of pricing control, complete liquidation and cash at the end of the sale is appealing.

Of course, the estate sale business is not all a bed of roses; it has challenges just like every other type of business. But low financial risk and fulfillment of a compelling social need sounds like a good business model to me.

Five Ways to Finance Your Antiques Business Without a Bank Loan

Applying for a bank loan for your fledgling antiques business is a quick and easy process: You fill out the loan application, and the bank says, "No!" It's sad but it's true. Bankers just don't understand the antiques trade. Unlike most bankable retail businesses, the antiques trade has no published operating benchmarks, too many variables in valuing inventory and is overwhelmingly undercapitalized.

These days, even well-established antiques retailers and auction houses can be turned down for a loan. Since the banking crisis of 2008, the standards for small business loans have become so stringent that 70 percent of all small business loans are turned down. It's no longer enough to have good credit and cash flow. In most cases, loan applicants must also have adequate collateral and show strong revenue growth and profitability for the past three years. How many antiques businesses do you know that have had strong revenue and profit growth in the past three years?

A loan officer can't make an exception for your loan just because you have been their customer for 30 years. Banking is a heavily regulated industry. A bank must adhere to its lending standards or federal regulators can fine them or shut them down. So, antiques dealers in need of a loan must seek funding sources outside of a bank. There are five choices that small businesses sometimes use for quick cash. Let's sort through the good, the bad, and the ugly of them to see what might make sense for your business.

Credit Cards

Okay — we're back to the bank. I mention this because it's the first place that many small business owners turn when they need cash quickly. Using credit cards to fund a business is a terrible idea. Credit card interest rates are subject to change, fees can be excessive, and the payoff period is open-ended. Dealers who abuse their credit cards will soon find themselves at a different bank: bankruptcy.

Social Lending

Social lending has moved beyond getting a loan from your Uncle Harry and sending him occasional payments. Virgin Money (owned by Sir Richard Branson's Virgin Group; you know, Virgin Records, Virgin Airlines, Virgin Mobile, etc.) will provide you and Uncle Harry with all the paperwork you need to make your loan "official." When the paperwork is done, Virgin will (for a small fee) service the loan, collect all the payments, and hold your feet to the fire if you don't pay on time.

Peer-to-Peer Lending

If you don't have an Uncle Harry with a few extra bucks, there is a new twist on social lending called Peer-to-Peer (P2P) lending. In P2P, lending clubs are formed and the members invest in and borrow from each other. Lenders and borrowers congregate at websites such as Lending-Club.com and Prosper.com. Borrowers request loans and are screened for credit, and investors purchase the notes created by the borrowers. Investors receive higher interest rates than they would get from most common investments, and borrowers get lower interest rates than they would get from a bank. Everyone wins.

Since the banking crisis of 2008, the standards for small business loans have become so stringent that 70 percent of all small business loans are turned down.

Applying for a P2P loan is a lot easier than applying for a bank loan. P2P applications can be done online in complete privacy and completed in just a few minutes. Usually, all that is required to qualify for a P2P loan is adequate income and the good credit of the borrower. In fact, the amount of money available to borrow and the interest rate that will be paid are tied directly to the borrower's credit rating.

Merchant Cash Advance

Antiques retailers and auction houses that take a lot of credit card payments find that a Merchant Cash Advance (MCA) can be used as a quick-cash solution. An MCA is an advance on future credit card receipts. Since it's not a loan, the qualification standards are different than they would be for a bank loan. Unlike the bank loan application process, a business does not have to produce tax returns, financial statements and a business plan in order to get an advance. There is no collateral required, and no requirement that the money be used for a particular purpose. Also, approval is not entirely based on the owner's personal credit score.

-In order to qualify for a Merchant Cash Advance, you must have:

-$2,500 minimum in credit card sales per month

-4 months as the current business owner

-Be current on the property lease

-A FICO score of at least 500 (better credit = more funds and lower rates)

The benefit of a Merchant Cash Advance:

1. There is no fixed payment; repayment of the advance is done from credit card receipts. When sales are down, the payment is low. When sales are up (and you can afford it), the payment goes up.

2. There is no fixed repayment term. The time it takes to repay the advance will vary according to credit card sales. A Merchant Cash Advance is cash flow friendly: You pay more in good months, less in slow months. Simple.

3. Interest is not charged on a Merchant Cash Advance; it can't be. Interest calculations are based on borrowing a fixed amount of money for a predetermined amount of time. Since a cash advance has neither fixed payment or fixed length of time, interest cannot be calculated. Instead, a portion of a business asset – credit card receivables – is being sold at a discount.

4. There are no personal guarantees. Of course, dealers who fraudulently enter into a Merchant Cash Advance are open to prosecution. For honest merchants who operate with integrity, a Merchant Cash Advance is a valuable financial tool.

A word of warning about Merchant Cash Advances: You're mortgaging your future cash flow. Make sure that the payback terms will leave you with enough future operating cash.

Retirement Funds

Both an individual 401K and a Roth IRA can be tapped for a business loan. What's nice about using retirement funds is that, in a strict sense, it is not a loan; it's your money. What's not so nice is that you risk losing your retirement.

An individual 401k loan is permitted using the accumulated balance of the individual 401k as collateral for the loan. Individual 401k loans can access up to half of the total balance of the 401k up to a maximum of $50,000. A loan from an individual 401k is received tax-free and penalty-free, provided that the loan payments are made on time. The monthly loan payments of principal and interest are repaid back into your own Individual 401k.

Roth IRA money can be accessed by choosing the self-directed option rather than having your banker invest the funds for you. With a self-directed IRA, an entrepreneur sets up a Limited Liability Corporation that holds the IRA account funds. As the primary investor, the IRA is the owner of the LLC, and the dealer acts as the directing member of the LLC. The directing member is free to invest the IRA funds however they please. All of the profits from the business stay in the LLC account, earning compound interest. The key word here is "profits". The expenses of operating the LLC – including a reasonable owner's salary and perks – are all deducted from operating income in order to determine profits.

Antiques dealers who need money for leasehold improvements or inventory purchases can sometimes find funds in one of the above five places. A final word of caution: Don't borrow money to cover operating expenses. If you can't pay your bills from the regular cash flow of your business, it's time to liquidate and close the doors.

Absolute Versus Reserve Auctions

The Uniform Commercial Code says you can retract a bid before a lot closes, but whether you're legally clear to back out depends on the auction

Okay, auction buffs, its pop quiz time!

Here's the scenario: You're at an auction, and the lot being offered is a Conoco sign. There are four primary bidders. Bidder A drops out at $200; Bidder B drops out at $300, and Bidders C and D drive the bidding up to $600. Bidder C then bids $650, but gets a sharp elbow in the ribs from his wife. Bidder C then frantically waves his arms saying, "I'm out, I withdraw my bid." The auctioneer should:

A. Refuse to release Bidder C from his bid because a bid is legally binding.

B. Release Bidder C from his bid and pick up the bidding with the next higher bid, Bidder D's bid for $600.

C. Start the bidding over from zero.

The correct answer is C: Start the bidding over from zero. The reason for this is found in the Uniform Commercial Code.

Although state auction rules vary slightly, all states (except Louisiana) base their auction law on the Uniform Commercial Code, or UCC. According to the UCC, (section 2-238 paragraph 3): "A bidder may retract his bid until the auctioneer's announcement of completion of the sale, but a bidder's retraction does not revive any previous bid."

I've heard auctioneers argue vehemently in favor of each of the three alternatives listed above. If some auctioneers aren't clear on the law, it's no wonder that the auction-going public is a little confused. Let's consider each alternative:

Are bids legally binding?

Whether a bid is legally binding depends on the type of auction. In the United States, the two primary types of auctions are "reserve" and "absolute." In a reserve auction, the seller has placed a minimum acceptable price on the item to be auctioned. In an absolute auction, the seller has agreed to sell for the highest bid, regardless of the amount offered.

The role of the auctioneer is to ratify the contract formed between the buyer and the seller. The UCC states, "the sale of an item is complete when the auctioneer so announces by the fall of the hammer or in other customary manner." In a reserve auction, the auctioneer is not authorized to sell for any amount below the reserve price. Any bids that are placed below the reserve cannot be ratified by the auctioneer; such bids are simply offers, and they are not binding. Bids above the reserve are binding, with the high bid ratified by the auctioneer when he declares the item sold.

In an absolute auction, the item offered must be sold to the highest bidder regardless of price. All bids are binding. Some auctioneers mistakenly believe that a bid for an item is just an offer, and that they can either accept the offer or reject it. I've seen auctioneers offer an item at "absolute sale" and then decline to sell the item because the bids offered didn't meet the auctioneer's expectations. Such a move is illegal. In an absolute auction, it's the auctioneer who offers the item for sale, the terms being "the highest bidder gets it regardless of the price." The auctioneer is legally bound to accept the highest bid.

If auctioneers aren't clear on the law, it's no wonder that the auction-going public is a little confused.

When the high bidder drops out, does the bidding start again at the second highest bid?

I've seen this tactic used occasionally by auctioneers, and it's illegal, as well. In the scenario offered above, the auctioneer would be wrong to say, "The last bid was $600; will you bid $625?" The price went up to $600 based on the competition between bidders C and D. Remove either of them from the competition and the price may never have gone that high. The auctioneer, therefore, is required to drop the price back to zero (or whatever the starting offer was) and then re-open the bidding. As the UCC says, "a bidder's retraction does not revive any previous bid."

Sharp auction bidders who know the law (UCC) can sometimes capitalize on sloppy auctioneering. By law, all auctions are considered to be reserve auctions unless they are declared to be absolute auctions. In other words, the default format for an auction is a reserve auction. Reserve auctions have minimum prices in order to protect sellers. Such price protection is to be guarded by the auctioneer, but sometimes an auctioneer will inadvertently throw away the price protection that the seller has instituted.

Take the above example, wherein the high bidder withdrew his bid. Suppose that the Conoco sign had a reserve price of $500. Suppose then that when the bidding reached $500, the auctioneer declared, "We now have an absolute auction!" I hear this regularly at auctions, and every time I do I cringe and hold my breath to see what will happen next. You see, the auctioneer has just announced that since the reserve price has been reached, the item will be sold to whoever is the high bidder. In an attempt to boost the bidding, he has declared an absolute auction.

However, that's a terrible move for the auctioneer, because he just took away all of the buyer's protections, and did so publicly (and in most cases, on videotape). When the high bidder withdrew his bid, all other bids bit the dust, and the bidding goes back to zero. The auctioneer changed the terms of the auction. Unless he specifically reinstates the reserve, the sign will be sold to the highest bidder. Since the auctioneer has announced that the Conoco sign is now being sold absolute, a bid of $1 would get the sign if $1 happened to be the highest bid. What would that mean for the seller? Well, the auctioneer would have to make up the difference between the high bid ($1) and the $500 reserve price. The auctioneer would owe the seller $499, minus whatever the selling fees on $500 would have been.

The Uniform Commercial Code section pertaining to auctions is short and sweet, just four paragraphs. It can be found here: http://tinyurl.com/CommercialCode.

Everyone who attends auctions regularly should become familiar with the section and its implications.

Do You Base Your Antiques Inventory Prices on Value, Cost or Gut Feelings?

Have you ever seen the Edvard Munch painting "The Scream?" If Munch doesn't ring a bell, recall the scene in the movie *Home Alone* in which Macaulay Culkin shaves for the first time, and then applies aftershave to his raw face: Hands slapped over his ears, eyes as big as saucers, he emits a scream that can be heard a block away.

Such was my response to a *Harvard Business Review* article that recently arrived in my inbox. The article discussed book pricing relative to Amazon's Kindle, Apple's iPad, and traditional print books. The author's position was to keep prices high for ebooks, because "charging what the market will bear creates value not just for companies but for consumers as well."

I read that statement and screamed. Macaulay has nothing on me.

You see, value is not created by price. Value is a personal issue. Price is determined by the intersection of supply and demand. Value can have an impact on demand, so consequently has some impact on price, but it is a secondary determinate. For example, I love baseball. When I was a kid, I was a big Washington Senators fan. I hold Senators memorabilia in high regard. If I personally value a Topps Camilo Pasqual baseball card at $20, then I would be willing to pay $20 or less for the card. If the intersection of supply and demand places the price of the card at $15, it doesn't mean that the card's value is $15, it just means that $15 is a good price for me, since it's below the value that I personally place on the card.

Antiques dealers rely on a variety of methods to determine the price of their wares; each dealer has his own "default" method of pricing. Some dealers price by "gut feel," some use price guides that list (last year's) average market price, some use online resources, and some use a "markup" method. Taken individually, these pricing models have more weaknesses than strengths. Taken together, they provide a good foundation for determining the value of an item – and hence it's best price. Let's look at how these three pricing strategies – research, cost (amount paid), and "gut feeling" – can combine to establish an item's best price.

It's been said that dealers make their money when they buy, not when they sell. A common trap for dealers is to overpay for items to which they attach a high personal value. I see this scenario played out often on the TV show "American Pickers." Mike loves his bicycles, Frank loves his oil cans, and sometimes they pay way too much for them. As they drive from town to town sorting through people's barns, they often buy based on "gut feeling" and research an item only when it's bought and in their van.

What is the lesson here? Research your purchases before you buy. Cell phone signals are available throughout most of America. In 2011, every dealer should be armed with a Smartphone, a cell phone data account, and subscriptions to several pricing databases. Pricing databases will provide a dealer with the historic points at which supply met demand – the starting point for determining what one should pay for an item (not sell it for).

Dealers who use a "markup" approach to pricing usually have a formula for their markup, two times the cost, three times the cost, etc. Though this method provides a quick "rule of thumb" for a dealer, it does not tie a dealer's profitability to the price of his products. A straight markup pricing formula does not allow for changes in expenses, so an uptick in expenses cuts right into a dealer's profits.

Look at it this way: If I've determined that I want to sell an item for at least three times my cost, my income statement might look like this:

Sales Revenue $300,000?
Cost of Goods Sold ($100,000)?
Operating Expenses ($140,000)
Profit $60,000

The following year, expenses go up, but I'm still using the "3 times" as my markup:

Sales Revenue $300,000
Cost of Goods Sold ($100,000)?
Operating Expenses ($165,000)
Profit $35,000

An 18 percent increase in expenses resulted in a 58 percent decrease in profits. The "3 times" markup did not take into account the upswing in expenses. If I want to maintain the same profit level in year two as in year one, I have to make sure that my price calculation includes both the higher expenses plus the return on investment that I want.

Here's how to do that: In year two, my operating expenses were equal to 165 percent of my cost of goods. Also, I want a 20 percent return on investment, just as I had in year one. If I have purchased an antique framistan for $100, here's how I'd calculate the selling price so that I make the desired profit:

Cost Of Goods $100
Operating Expense $165
($100 x 1.65)
Total Investment $265 ?
20% Return on Investment **$53**
Selling price $318

Or, in this example, you can multiply your cost by 3.18 times and be assured profitability. Two concepts are important here: Don't cheat yourself when it comes to your return on investment, and always know what your expenses are as a percentage of your cost of goods. This system is a variation of cost-plus pricing.

The weakness of cost-plus pricing is that it doesn't take into account market prices. When you calculate price based on what you pay, you could be either under or over the "intersection of supply and demand." The other weakness is that it doesn't take into account value. Determining value is where a dealer's "gut instinct" comes into play.

As in my baseball card analogy, value is what your customer believes an item is worth to them. If you know your customers and keep good records, you will know "who collects what" and have a record of their purchases. You should also know what criteria your customers use to make buying decisions (value markers).

Value is not created by price. Value is a personal issue. Price is determined by the intersection of supply and demand.

When you buy an item that has special appeal to one of your collectors, don't price via your standard markup. Determine how much you think your customer would be willing to pay, and price the item accordingly. Price high; you can always come down but you can never go up.

The psychology that drives value pricing also drives auction bidding: Items are worth more to some people than they are to others. The people who value an item the most are the ones who bid the highest for the item. Value pricing that is supported by research and cost analysis will bring a dealer the best price on the items in his inventory.

Dealers, take the time to review how much return you expect from your business, and analyze your expenses and your pricing structure. You'll be glad you did. That is, unless I have already sent you screaming from the room.

The Power of Stories is No Tall Tale

As a "follicularly challenged" gentleman, I take comfort in my collection of hats. Not for their collectible value mind you, but for their value in keeping my head warm and dry during the winter season.

As I'm so practical about my hats, I just had to smile when I read of the recent auction sale — for $14,160 — of the baseball cap worn by Neil Armstrong after the splashdown of Apollo 11. The cap's buyer paid more than 70,000 percent more for Armstrong's cap than I have ever paid for one of mine (usually about $20).

Would Armstrong's cap keep the sun out of my eyes any better than my tried-and-true "Key West, FL" cap? Probably not. What made the cap worth five figures to the buyer? Bragging rights.

The cap has zero intrinsic value: Would you wear a $14,000 cap to mow the lawn? No. The collector will display this cap prominently in his home as a testament to his own shrewdness. The buyer didn't walk on the moon, but he owns Armstrong's cap and will forever be associated with the name Neil Armstrong through the provenance of the cap.

And that's as it should be; $14,000 should buy a lot of bragging rights. Bragging rights is what the auctioneer was selling, and bragging rights is what the buyer was buying.

So, dealers: What do you sell in your shop? Investments, as in: "This collectible has been going up in price for years, and if you buy it you will certainly get a good return on your investment?" Or, are you selling commodities, as in, "I paid $100 for this and need to get three times my cost to make a profit." No matter how much you sell your item for, you can be sure that the buyer will take it home, display it and show it off to all his guests. He bought bragging rights.

What makes bragging rights valuable? It's the quality of the story attached to the object. Collectors love to tell stories about the items they have collected. Too often, the stories they tell are based on their own research and knowledge of the subject. Why is that? Shouldn't the buyer have heard the item's stories from the dealer who sold it?

The difference between Neil Armstrong's cap and a collectible from your shop is the quality of the story that is attached to the item. The better the story, the higher the item's value to a collector. Stories create value (don't confuse value with price; value is a personal issue; price is the intersection of supply and demand).

Consistently and enthusiastically shared stories will help your business in the following ways:

You can create brand awareness for your shop. Antique dealers are notorious for their "sameness." It's very difficult to differentiate your business from your competitor's when your inventories are similar and in constant flux. Having stories about the origins of your business and the provenance of your inventory will set you apart from your competitors.

You can create additional value in the minds of your shoppers if you enthusiastically share stories about the merchandise. Adding brief stories to your online product descriptions (or a link to a blog post or webpage containing the story) will help you sell more online.

The difference between Neil Armstrong's cap and a collectible from your shop is the quality of the story attached to the item. Want your inventory to sell itself? Share its stories.

You can sell more inventory at higher prices in your shop.

Mark Satterfield, author of *Unique Sales Stories: How to Get More Referrals, Differentiate Yourself from the Competition and Close More Sales through the Power of Stories* says that a good story goes beyond merely educating your customers about your merchandise.

"As I learned from hard-won experience," says Satterfield, "simply educating people about what I did wasn't enough. In order to be remembered, I needed to make my services come alive through the use of unique sales stories."

Fair enough. Speakers throughout recorded history have employed storytelling to get their point across. But, as Mr. Satterfield asks: "Why are some people so good at this while others are so painfully bad?" In a word: preparation.

We've all seen musicians who make playing an instrument seem effortless, and athletes who ably glide across the playing field. What we don't see is the years of practice and training they went through in order to acquire their skills. Storytelling is an acquired skill, and, like all other skills, it must be practiced if we are to master it. Let's take some tips from Mr. Satterfield about how to improve our storytelling skills:

What's the point you wish to make? Begin your story with the end in mind. If you want to make the point that your family has been in the antiques business for generations, don't just say, "My family has been in the antiques business for generations." Tell the story about how your great-grandfather started selling railroad keepsakes to the folks back East when he was laying tracks for the transcontinental railroad back in the 1860s. Or whatever.

Target your audience. Your readers and listeners should see themselves (their aspirations and their hobbies) reflected in your stories.

Create sympathetic characters. If your customer is reluctant to buy because of price, tell a story about a customer of yours who was at first reluctant to buy (had the same problem) but later was thrilled with his purchase (formula: feel/felt/found: "I know how you feel. Last week, Mr. Collector was in here and said he felt the same way you do. He made the purchase anyway, and let me tell you what he found.").

Be your authentic self.

Practice.

One thing is certain: The one element that separates you from your competitors is your stories. No one has your stories but you. The stories that you choose to share will reveal your personality to your customers. An antiques business is built on trust, and customers like to know who you are and what your background is before they decide if they can trust you. Storytelling is a great way to build the bridge of trust. To dealers who are already employing this technique, I doff my hat.

Next Time, Try Negotiating – Not Haggling

"You saved $36 today!" exclaimed the clerk at JC Penny's. "Gee, that's great!" I replied. "I spent $31 and saved $36! What a deal!"

These days, corporate retailers love to tell me how much I saved while shopping at their store: They tell me when I buy groceries, and when I buy hardware. I was even reminded of how much I "saved" the last time I got my car serviced. Sometimes, they even print the savings amount on my receipt so that I'll be reminded of what great folks they are when I reconcile my checkbook.

The crux of the matter for me is that I don't really care how much I saved; I care how much I spent.

Who believes anymore that retail prices actually reflect what the seller expects to get for his merchandise? It's been known for decades that the asking price for homes and automobiles is fiction. For the past five years, retailers in almost every category have been training us that their asking price is fiction as well.

Of course, we in the antiques and second-hand trade have always known that the asking price is not the "real" price. We haggle over price when we buy and we haggle over price when we sell. Haggling is "business as usual" for antiques dealers. But, is haggling good business? In my opinion, it's not. I prefer to negotiate, and there's a big difference between haggling and negotiating. Haggling is all about price; negotiating is about an exchange of value.

I found it enlightening to learn that the Latin roots of the word "haggle" literally mean "to hack" or "to cut unevenly." Doesn't that describe the typical haggling scenario: The buyer hacking away at the seller's price, while the seller tries to defend his price position? The Latin roots of the word "negotiation," however, are less objectionable: "neg," which is to say "not," and "otium," meaning leisure. In other words, negotiation is not leisure, it's business. I guess the Romans really didn't mix business with pleasure.

What advantage does negotiating have over haggling? As a dealer, negotiating puts you back in the game. In a haggle, the customer knows that you have overhead to pay and that you want his money. But, what do you know about your customer? Unless you know why your customer is interested in buying an item, you have no negotiating position. All you can do is dig in and defend your price.

Arthur Murray taught me how to negotiate from a seller's perspective. Not the actual Arthur Murray, but the manager of one of his franchised dance studios. Back in the late 1970s my wife and I signed up for a "six ballroom dancing lessons for $10" introductory package at Arthur Murray. At the end of each half-hour private lesson, the teacher had us fill out a questionnaire and give feedback about the class: Would we like to have dancing be part of our lives, did we have the time for lessons, could we afford it, and so on. In short, the questionnaire covered every possible objection we might later offer as to why we didn't want to sign a contract for a more expensive dance class. When the time came for the sales pitch, I was dead meat.

The crux of the matter is that I don't really care how much I saved; I care how much I spent.

The lesson in negotiating was worth the price of the dance class. Plus, I can now do a respectable Fox Trot when called upon to do so at weddings and such.

In order to turn a haggle into a negotiation, you have to find out what value the customer finds in your offering. That's exactly what the manager at Arthur Murray did: They asked a lot of questions and engaged me in conversation.

You can determine how much your customer values your item by engaging them in conversation and walking them through what I call the "Value Funnel." The Value Funnel is a series of questions that allows you to uncover how much the customer wants your item. You can adapt these questions to your particular circumstance, but I prefer to use them in this order:

1. What types of things do you collect?
2. What are your favorite items in your collection?
3. How long have you been collecting (item)?
4. Where do you find your (items)?
5. Why would you want to add (your inventory item) to your collection?
6. Would you like me to wrap that one up for you?

Of course, the last question is just an opening to begin the negotiation. If he's interested, he will move to haggling over the price. You, however, have armed yourself with what you need to transform the haggling into a negotiation: You know what he collects, what his favorites are, and why he wants to add your item to his collection.

The above questions will help you to determine how much the customer values your offering, and that knowledge increases your negotiating position. If you're selling a Victorian occasional table, your customer may have indicated that she has "just the perfect spot" for the table. If your customer collects antique metal toys, your item may be what he needs to complete a set. Either way, you can now talk about something other than price — and that's the difference between a haggle and a negotiation.

Once you are negotiating, there are a few other things you can do to move the discussion away from price:

-Change the quantity; if your markup will allow, throw in another similar item, or another item at half price.

-Change the terms; for example, on a large piece of furniture offer 30, 60, or 90 days same as cash.

-Offer to deliver the item.

-Offer a bonus that has nothing to do with the item, like tickets to a movie or event or a gift certificate to a restaurant.

The important point to remember in any negotiation is that whoever wants to make the deal the most has the upper hand. Price is not the only point under consideration. In your store, you should be the one to set the terms of any negotiation. When you negotiate rather than haggle, both you and your customer benefit. And then you don't have to remind him how much money he saved in order to turn him into a regular customer.

How Smart Check Policies Protect Antiques Businesses

T he 2011 hubbub surrounding William Meloy's use of bad checks to scam antique stores caught me off guard. In these days of electronic check verification, Internet check processing, and point-of-sale terminals that support multiple payment options, I was surprised at how easily Meloy victimized the dealers.

For those who missed the story, the grandfatherly Meloy allegedly spent his summer defrauding antique stores in Wyoming, Missouri, North Dakota, and Minnesota before he was finally arrested in Great Falls, Mont. Writing checks on a closed account, Meloy would make purchases in the neighborhood of $1,000 and then resell the goods for cash to other antique dealers.

As I read the news reports and listened to comments from the defrauded dealers, the refrain, "He seemed like such a sweet guy" dominated the responses. Of course, building trust is key to a conman's operation. I'm reminded of the story of Frank Abagnale, the teenage conman who, back in the 1960s, cashed over $2.5 million worth of forged checks before he turned 21. How did he do this? He masqueraded as an airline pilot, a doctor, a lawyer, and a professor as he cashed the bad checks. People trusted him. He had such an engaging manner that a former Houston Chief of Police said: "Frank Abagnale could write a check on toilet paper, drawn on the Confederate States Treasury, sign it 'U.R. Hooked,' and cash it at any bank in town, using a Hong Kong driver's license for identification."

None of us are immune from fraud. Back in the early 1990s, I was victimized by a con artist. We called him "Doctor Bob," an alleged chiropractor who was in town to buy a well-known restaurant. Within 30 days, he had conned me along with the former restaurant owner, the landlord, the State Liquor Board, his suppliers, the city police, and about two dozen employees. He left town with a lot of money. Fortunately, I got my property back.

Building trust is also a key element in building a good antiques business. Customers have to trust that you are representing your goods honestly, and you, in return, have to exhibit a certain amount of trust in your customers. So, put a dealer wanting to make a sale and gain a new customer together with a conman and you have a recipe for trouble.

Conmen are smart to target small businesses because a small business isn't likely to have the latest electronic safeguards. Most antiques businesses are decidedly low-tech compared to big retailers like Sears and Wal-Mart. So I wonder: What are a dealer's defenses against a conman with an engaging smile and friendly manner? And, are the costs of high-tech safeguards worth the investment for dealers who have had very few issues with bad checks?

Put a dealer wanting to make a sale and gain a new customer together with a conman and you have a recipe for trouble.

The truth is, today's con artists are smart and technologically sophisticated. Personal computers, scanners and color photocopiers are accessible everywhere. No matter how careful you are, you can be defrauded, and not just by accepting bad checks: The checks you write are also at risk. Blank checks taken from your checkbook, canceled checks found in your trash, or checks you mail to pay your bills are all useful to a con artist.

Ultimately, all you can do (short of installing an expensive electronic check verification system) is to have a sound check acceptance policy, know the telltale signs of a bad check, and keep track of the checks that you write. Here are a few things for you to think about:

Know what your actual check losses are. If your losses are anywhere near the cost of an electronic check verification system (usually 2 to 3 percent of sales), then your solution is simple: Go electronic.

Set your parameters for check acceptance. Will you have a dollar limit? What forms of identification are acceptable? Will you accept third-party checks or business checks? How about payroll checks?

Know the signs of a high-risk check. They include:

1. The check lacks perforations. Checks made on a copier will be sliced along the edge; checks from a book will have a perforated edge.

2. The check number is either missing or is low. Most bad checks are written on accounts less than one year old.

3. The font used to print the customer's name is different from the font used to print the address, or appears to have been written using a typewriter.

4. The check has missing information, like the customer's address or the bank's address.

5. Wrong information, such as the check number at the end of the routing number not matching the check number.

6. Stains or discolorations on the check that might indicate washing (using acetone to erase ink)

7. The bank routing numbers are shiny (the magnetic ink used on valid checks is dull in appearance).

8. There are stamps or other markings in the "Memo" line or on the back of the check.

Have a camera installed at your checkout counter. Crooks don't like to have their picture taken.

If your bank offers checks with security features, use them. Recently revised Uniform Commercial Code regulations state that if a fraud is committed that could have been avoided by a business using secure checks, and your bank offers such secure checks, then your business must share responsibility for the loss.

When in doubt, do a quick Internet search of the name and address of the check issuer. One of Meloy's victims did a search after his check bounced, and found out that he was wanted in several states. Had she done the search before she accepted his check, she would still have her merchandise.

There are William Meloys, Frank Abagnales and Doctor Bobs everywhere. Dealers who have a sound check acceptance policy, know the signs of a bad check, and stay alert are less likely to fall victim to fraud than dealers who casually accept checks.

If you'd like to check your vulnerability to check fraud, the website Fake-Checks.org has six fun "fraud tests" that you can take, along with fraud prevention training videos and a list of common scams.

How to Be the Antiques Dealer Who Knows Something About Art

"Antiques dealers don't know anything about art," explained the art gallery owner. "You have to be really careful buying art from an antiques dealer because you never know what you're going to get." I didn't argue with the woman because I knew from my own experience that what she said about antiques dealers and art is generally true. Some of my best art purchases have been from antiques dealers and auctioneers who didn't know the value of what they had. So, I didn't defend antiques dealers to the gallery owner.

In practice, antiques dealers who are knowledgeable and well inventoried in art generally represent their shops as art galleries that specialize in art and decorative antiques. Antiques and collectibles dealers, on the other hand, usually carry art as an afterthought. Often, the art on their walls was acquired in an estate buyout rather than purchased as individual items. Most antiques dealers offer some type of art for sale, but many dealers shy away from art because they don't know enough to profit from it.

Antiques dealers who have found that their large furniture items aren't selling would do well to remember that most rooms have more wall space than floor space. The good news for antiques dealers is that they can profit handsomely from the everyday, run-of-the-mill unsigned art they find at estate sales, garage sales, and auctions.

It is not necessary to be knowledgeable about signed, collectible art or investment-grade art. To make a profit selling art in an antique shop, dealers need to know two things: what most people buy, and the differences between paintings and prints.

What Most People Buy

As a rule, the general public doesn't know anything about art, either. When I worked as an art auctioneer, hardly a day went by that I didn't hear a customer say, "I don't know anything about art, but I know what I like." Indeed, what they really mean is that they like what they know! What people know and like is artwork that captures their attention and that resonates emotionally with them. That's why artists like Thomas Kinkade have sold millions of dollars worth of nostalgia prints.

Ron Davis, in his book, *The Art Dealers Field Guide*, suggests that an artwork's size and subject matter have a direct impact on its salability. Let's look at what Mr. Davis has to say: "When it comes to size, bigger is better, and for big artwork horizontal beats vertical. Interior decorators will generally place artwork on a wall above furniture. When buying artwork for your inventory, visualize how the size of the art will look placed over various sizes of furniture. Sofas are typically 60 inches wide, so artwork that is 4 to 5 feet wide are in demand. The standard room ceiling height is 8 feet, and sofas and chairs are roughly 3 feet high, so artwork that is 3 to 4 feet tall fits nicely above a chair or sofa.

Antiques dealers whose large furniture items aren't selling would do well to remember that most rooms have more wall space than floor space.

Of course, artworks of all sizes are sold, and often the size and shape of the artwork is determined by the work's subject matter. Here's what Davis says about subject matter: "Women are more valuable than men. Images of young girls sell better than images of young boys, and looks count. Male or female, the subject must have clearly defined handsome or pretty features."

There is more demand for landscapes than there is for seascapes. Open landscapes with rivers or lakes sell better than interior, forested landscapes. Living things (flowers, fruit, and people) will outsell images of inanimate objects (tools, furniture). Pictures of domestic animals (dogs, kittens, horses) will move faster than pictures of wild animals (again, it's the emotional connection; people care about their pets). One exception, according to Ron Davis, is cows. For some reason, cows aren't big sellers, especially to those who had to get up at 4 a.m. to milk them.

More is better than less: A flower arrangement is preferable to a single flower and a bowl of fruit is preferable to one apple. Also, bright colors sell better than pastels, thick paint sells better than thin watercolors, day scenes are preferred to night scenes, and happy subjects are preferred to sad subjects. This is mostly common sense. Before you buy an artwork for your inventory, ask yourself how it would look from across a room: Would a houseguest be able to tell what it is, and not frown?

Let me add a caveat to the above paragraph: My experience has shown that if you're in a "tourist" town, visitors will always want a reminder of their visit. Visitors to Annapolis, Md., love images of crab boats, and visitors to Ketchikan, Ark., will take home images of wolves and eagles. Also, collectors of historical memorabilia will buy almost anything that is representative of their favorite subject.

Five Basic Artistic Techniques

Of course, artists and dealers will be shocked by my limited presentation. However, my objective here is to suggest ways that you, the antique dealer, can make money selling art in your shop. To do so you need to at least know what technique you're looking at. If you were a wine salesman, you would only embarrass yourself by calling a white wine a red wine. Knowing the difference between the four basic artistic techniques is almost as simple as telling red wine from white wine.

Paintings

Often, people refer to any framed artwork as a "painting." We know that that's not the case. Too many times, I've been baited into surveying an estate by the promise of a great collection of "paintings," only to find a collection of worthless, poorly framed poster prints. Here's how you can identify a painting: It has paint on it. Duh. If it doesn't have paint, it's not a painting. The public perception is that paintings are more valuable than prints. As we shall see, that's not always the case but all things being equal, unsigned estate paintings can be priced higher than similar prints.

Four Types of Prints

The ready availability of four-color offset lithography has given art prints a bad name. I have often admired a nice artwork only to have my host apologize and say "It's just a print." Really? I would love to have a thousand-year-old Japanese woodcut, a Rembrandt etching, a Chagall lithograph, or a Warhol serigraph: all are prints. Prints can be a real moneymaker if you know how to correctly identify them.

Dealers should be able to know the difference between and correctly identify the following: woodcuts, etchings, lithographs, and serigraphs (I'm counting giclees as a type of serigraph).

Trust me, this isn't hard to do. A detailed explanation of each technique is beyond the scope of this section, but detailed explanations and demonstrations can be found by searching Google and YouTube for each technique. You will be rewarded for your effort.

Antiques dealers can acquire unsigned estate artworks dirt-cheap and sell them for a nice profit if they know what people are buying and what to call each type of artwork. Art dealers will still have a "leg up" when it comes to a knowledge of art, but I'll bet their cash register won't ring as often.

How the Antiques Business Can Capture Gen X

Today, the antiques business has a new problem: old customers. Baby Boomers and their parents, who have been collecting antiques for decades, no longer have the room or the inclination to buy more antiques. Their Generation X successors do not seem to care for antiques.

"The trend is away from antiques," says Red Whaley, owner of an antiques business in Forney, Texas, since 1968. "I think it skips a generation," Whaley said in a recent Associated Press article. "You just do not want what your parents had."

Attend any antiques show in the United States and all you will see is a sea of silver hair and bald heads. This leaves antiques dealers in a quandary: Their customer base is shrinking, sales are plummeting, and they are buried in inventory.

The shrinking customer base is just phase one of the problem. When millions of boomers start to downsize and the antiques they have been collecting for decades hit the resale market, prices will plunge as well.

There will be an overabundance of supply, and very little demand. Boomers that bought antiques as an investment are in for a rude awakening. In many cases, they will not recoup their original investment.

The antiques trade has tried everything to hook new buyers: scotch tastings, seminars, door prizes, and even handwritten invitations. Little progress has been made in capturing the pocketbooks of Gen X.

Why are they not buying? I think that Richard Whaley, Red's son, hit the nail on the head when he said, "It is more functional now. We sell a lot of (decorative) mailboxes."

Functional: That is the key word

I have often been told by Gen Xers that they do not buy antique furniture because it does not fit the needs of modern technology. An antique flat-top desk has no place to run computer cords, store CDs, or comfortably place a monitor and keyboard.

Old wooden office chairs are not ergonomic and one cannot sit in them for hours at a time. Even starter apartments have walk-in closets that make armoires obsolete.

The twin essentials of furniture making have always been form and function, or beauty and usability. For Boomers and their parents, furniture was for sitting, eating, or sleeping. Simple functions.

> **Gen X buyers will not completely furnish their homes with antiques as their parents have done, but the market for accessories and occasional pieces will continue to be strong.**

For the Boomer antiques collector, beauty of form lent an added dimension to the simple functions of furniture. Function was a given.

Boomers bought because the form was beautiful. For Gen Xers, the opposite is true. For them, furniture provides a place to eat, sleep, sit, play video games, and sit for hours at a workstation for work or socializing.

Function takes precedence over form. The furniture has to perform. Beautiful antiques that do not function well in the Gen X lifestyle are an impediment. Why would they buy them? For Gen X, buying decisions are made on the basis of performance, not beauty.

How, then, do we sell to Gen X buyers?

We stop trying to sell beauty and investment as our primary sales pitches. This is easiest to do with accessories and occasional pieces.

Sell function first, then beauty, and then investment. Functionally, a lamp is a lamp. An antique lamp will work as well as a new lamp, plus it has the added benefits of being unique, beautiful, and a good investment. See what I mean? Start by selling function.

You cannot use that approach with a roll top desk. It is not functional in terms of the Gen X lifestyle. What does that mean for your business? Re-evaluate your inventory. If an item is not functional for the Gen X buyer, liquidate it or you will soon find yourself with a store full of inventory you cannot sell. Start buying inventory with Gen-X functionality in mind, and eliminate anything that does not fit that profile.

Gen X buyers will not completely furnish their homes with antiques as their parents have done but the market for accessories and occasional pieces will continue to be strong.

As an added bonus, these smaller pieces are easily shipped. That makes them ideal candidates for online selling, which is where Gen X does a lot of its buying anyway.

Generation X facts

-Generation X, abbreviated to Gen X, was born after the Baby Boom, with earliest birth dates ranging from about 1960 to the latest at about 1980.

-Generation X makes up about 20 percent of the U.S. population and has more education.

-Generation Xers are generally between 52 and 32 years old.

-Gen Xer's income is progressively higher than the previous generation because more women are in the workplace, according to a 2007 study.

Can Your Antiques Appraisals Land You in Court?

A ntiques dealers have exposure from two sources: attorneys and the IRS.

It's unlikely that a dealer will be sued over an appraisal unless the amount involved is substantial; there has to be enough money involved to pay a lawyer and have something left over. Risk for a dealer is directly proportional to the value of the item.

It's well established that one of the root causes of the recent U.S. banking crisis was over-inflated and poorly researched property and housing appraisals. Poor appraisals that resulted in a financial crisis are not new: Faulty appraisals were also at the root of the Savings and Loan failures of the 1980s and 1990s. In both crises, loans were made on the basis of appraised value. When a property's appraised value was overstated and the loan went bad, there was not enough actual value in the property to collateralize the loan.

Poorly executed personal property appraisals can result in negative fallout as well. Estate executors who rely on appraisals to settle an estate can be sued by heirs; property owners can suffer loss from either over-payment of insurance premiums or under-insurance based on an appraisal; and taxpayers who use an appraisal to justify a tax deduction may face stiff fines if the appraisal is overstated or rejected outright. Anyone who offers appraisal services — including antique dealers — must be able to defend the appraisals that they give.

Antiques dealers perform appraisals on a regular basis in their shops, at appraisal fairs, and at promotional events. How much liability and exposure does a dealer have for the appraisals that they perform? What must a dealer do to defend himself against potential lawsuits regarding his written appraisals?

Dealers have exposure from two sources: attorneys and the IRS.

The US has 70 percent of the world's lawyers, roughly one lawyer for every 200 people. None of them get paid unless they successfully sue someone. We are a litigious society.

It's unlikely that a dealer will be sued over an appraisal unless the amount involved is substantial; there has to be enough money involved to pay a lawyer and have something left over. Risk for a dealer is directly proportional to the value of the item.

A more serious concern for dealers is the IRS. A dealer-appraiser who prepares an incorrect appraisal can be subject to a penalty under Section 6662 of the tax code if:

-He knows, or should have known, that the appraisal will be used in a tax return or claim for refund, and

-The appraisal results in either the 20 percent or 40 percent overstatement penalty to the taxpayer.

When performing a tax appraisal, the risk to a dealer lies in providing a value that is more than 20 percent too high.

An offending appraiser can be fined up to $1,000 and may be permanently barred from submitting tax appraisals to the IRS. In addition, the appraiser may be subject to civil penalties.

The 'Ten Commandments' of a Dealer Appraisal

When asked to give an appraisal, a dealer must first ask himself if he knows enough about a particular item to qualify as an expert. It's not enough to know what sort of price tag he might put on an item in his shop; he must actually have reached a level of connoisseurship for the item. Don't attempt to give a valuation where no connoisseurship exists.

Anyone who offers appraisal services — including antique dealers — must be able to defend the appraisals that they give.

The public generally accepts that value can be established through the informed opinion of an expert. Smart consumers know that opinions vary, so they may ask two or three "experts" to value their item before arriving at a value conclusion. Consumers often assume that the opinion offered by an antique dealer constitutes a valid appraisal. Nothing could be further from the truth, and therein lays the problem for dealers: An appraisal that will stand up in tax and civil courts must meet the requirements of the Uniform Standards of Professional Appraisal Practice (USPAP). Few antique dealers are trained in USPAP.

Dealers can easily avoid disappointing their customers and stay out of trouble with tax and court authorities by following some simple guidelines when they write an appraisal. The guidelines are:

1. If you are charging for the appraisal, write everything down. Otherwise, you may find yourself in a "he said, she said" argument in the future. If you're not charging, don't give them anything at all in writing.

2. Don't call your valuation an appraisal; doing so opens the door for trouble. In real estate, mortgage companies pursuing a home foreclosure rely on the value opinion of real estate brokers rather than a costly appraisal. The value so presented is called a Broker's Price Opinion (BPO); the name clearly says this is not an appraisal it's a broker's opinion of value. Find a word that suits you other than appraisal and use that instead.

3. Write the date of the valuation. You'd be surprised how often dealers leave this out.

4. Clearly identify the person who is paying for the valuation. If your customer sells the item the following week and the new owner decides to use your valuation to substantiate a tax deduction, you may have a problem.

5. Identify the intended use of the valuation. If the customer tells you that they want to sell the item on Craigslist and then they use your valuation to substantiate a tax deduction, you may have a problem.

6. Identify the type of value; i.e., market value, auction value, retail value, and replacement value. Value is circumstantial, and the value of items may

change. On *Antiques Roadshow*, the appraisers are generally careful to define the value they place on objects. You will hear, "I believe this item would bring $X at auction," or "In my shop I would put a retail price of $X on this item."

7. Identify your market area. An item may be worth more in New York City than in Harlan, Ky.

8. Write a good description of the item: brand, serial number, markings, material, and anything else that helps you arrive at a value.

9. Take good photographs.

10. Add a short paragraph that tells who you are and why you are qualified to make the valuation.

These 10 items can easily be presented fill-in-the-blank style on a single page.

USPAP-compliant appraisals have strict requirements that are much more detailed than the above suggestions. Dealers can avoid the complications resulting from a "too casual" approach to appraisals if they will clearly identify the item and state that they are providing their opinion of an item's value to a certain individual for a particular purpose on a stated date and for a stated place (market).

How Managing Your Antiques Inventory Can Cut Your Taxes

I t's often said that two of life's certainties are death and taxes. What's said less often — but is just as certain — is that your tax liabilities can be the death of your business.

You work hard to create profits so you can re-invest those profits into inventory to build your business. Then, when the time comes to pay the IRS, you have no cash because it's all tied up in your inventory.

The last time I checked, the IRS didn't accept Victorian rockers or Depression glass as payment for tax liabilities — they actually wanted cash. To make sure that you have enough cash when tax time comes, you need to get a good handle on your inventory.

For non-accountants, here's a look at how inventory and taxes are related (to keep it simple, let's assume that there were no returns and that no inventory purchases were made): Net Sales minus Cost of Goods Sold equals Gross Profit.

There are several ways of calculating the cost of the goods you sell, but the most commonly used is to subtract your inventory on hand at the end of an accounting period from your inventory on hand at the beginning of an accounting period. Missing from the ending inventory will be the items you have sold plus items that were stolen, misplaced, not counted, given away, or otherwise unaccounted for. If you miss counting $5,000 worth of inventory (for example, a packed show trailer that you missed) then your Cost of Goods Sold will be $5,000 too high and your profit $5,000 too low. You will have understated your profits and underpaid your taxes. The amount of cash you have in the bank will seem disproportionately high to the profit you are showing and you may think that you are flush with cash.

If you are like many retailers, you'll spend the "extra" cash. When you account for the "missing" inventory the following month, you won't have the cash to catch up on the extra tax liability.

The first step to controlling your inventory is to know exactly what information you need to track to create maximum sales and profits with minimum tax liability.

To avoid overpaying or underpaying your taxes, you need to control and track your inventory. The first step to controlling your inventory is to know exactly what information you need to track to create maximum sales and profits with minimum tax liability. Inventory tracking is what we're going to investigate here today.

A good inventory system is more than just a list of what items you have and how much you paid for them. An adequate tracking system will allow you to do the following:

-"Take inventory" quickly and easily: If you have a large inventory, counting everything can be time consuming. An inventory system that utilizes a bar code scanner is a great time saver. There are barcode-reading scanners available such as KwikCountEX that are relatively inexpensive and download their information directly to your Excel spreadsheets.

-Craft better tags: Turn your price tags into a silent sales force.

-Know the location of every item: If you only have one retail location, this isn't a big issue. But, if you have multiple retail locations, a warehouse and keep trucks and trailers loaded for shows, then your inventory program should show you where everything is located so that it can be counted when you take inventory.

-Inventory turnover by category: This will tell you at a glance what kinds of items are selling briskly so you can keep these items stocked. Also, you will be able to identify items that took a long time to sell. If it took you three years to sell a widget, then that should be a clear sign that you shouldn't stock any more widgets.

-Aging of specific items or categories: With this point, we get back to the tax issue.

According to GAAP (generally accepted accounting principles) inventory can be valued at the lower of cost or market value. For example, if you have a store full of Victorian or mahogany furniture that you've had for several years, you're only hurting yourself by keeping it on your books at the price you paid for it. Clearly, the market has dropped for these items and in many instances they may not be worth what you paid. If this is the case, the items should be marked down.

Doing so will have both a positive and a negative effect: Your cost of goods sold will rise and your profits will go down, but because your profits are lower, your taxes will be lower (see your accountant for details). The net result of this move is that you will have more cash in your pocket. You can still sell the furniture for your original retail price (if you can get it) and you'll re-capture the markdown when the item is sold. In the meantime, you'll pay less in taxes.

Although specialty inventory software programs are available, I've found that the most flexible software for keeping track of inventory is Microsoft Excel. Excel is widely supported, can be customized, is expandable, and uploads easily to eBay and e-stores.

If you keep your books and business plan on Excel spreadsheets, your Excel inventory sheets can be linked directly to them, as well.

Here's a list of basic column headings for an Excel inventory worksheet. Add more as needed, but start by using these; doing so will help you to stay profitable and keep your tax liabilities under control.

-Inventory Number (so you can differentiate similar items). Consider coding your price flexibility into your inventory number for easier negotiating: Date In, Item, Location, Description. Read more: *Antique Trader's* "Behind the Gavel" column, "How to get search engines to notice your antiques inventory descriptions."

-Provenance (see "Crafting Better Tags"), Condition, Category (eBay lists 22 categories of antiques; I recommend that you use those for easier online selling), Sold Date, Sold Location, Payment Form (credit card, PayPal, cash), Photos.

-Over time, you will determine what information you need to know to run your business effectively. Columns can be added as you need them. I prefer Excel because I can change it as my needs change rather than shop for new accounting software every two years.

Lastly, a disclaimer: I'm not a certified public accountant. If you have accounting or tax questions, discuss your specific situation with an accountant. All I have done here is share my experience (and many others have had the same experience).

Now a rejoinder: Don't let your accountant run your business. Accountants can supply you with financial tools but it's up to you to use the tools as you see fit.

Section 3:
You Own Two Addresses: Your Shop and Your Website

Antiques Dealers Can Master Web Marketing

Yesterday's tools don't work very well in modern applications. Take a rotary phone, for example: It can still make phone calls, but it won't work outdoors, it won't connect to the Internet, and it won't take photos. A few of you are now saying, "I just want a telephone that makes phone calls." I'd be willing to bet that it's these same few who have said, "Internet marketing doesn't work." It's not that Internet marketing doesn't work. It's that they are taking a new tool (the Internet) and using it like it's an old tool. It's like owning an iPhone and using it like it's a rotary phone. They're not using the tool to its full advantage.

Much has been said lately about finding new customers and reaching a new generation of buyers. If you want to reach a new generation of buyers, you have to send your message to the place where new buyers are listening and approach them in the manner in which they prefer to be approached. Instead of searching for a silver bullet that will magically reach new customers on your terms, it's important to study when and how your potential customers prefer to receive advertising messages.

Demographics is Dead

For decades, companies have depended on demographics to target their advertising messages. But, demographics aren't as powerful as they used to be. As U.S. society has evolved, sub-groups have emerged within the traditional demographic groups. Our market has fragmented to the point where the old demographic tools are useless. New tools are needed if we are going to define our market and reach new customers. Those tools are available, and they all revolve around interactive social media marketing.

'Interactive' is the New Marketing Buzzword

Businesses are engaging new customers where the new customers live: on social networking sites like Facebook and Twitter. Once engaged, they approach their newfound customers to make purchases through email marketing. The marketing company Exact Target recently published research that shows:

- 93 percent of online consumers ("Subscribers") receive on average one permission-based marketing email per day

- 38 percent of online consumers ("Fans") have "liked," or become a follower of, at least one company on a social networking site. (For example, find *Antique Trader* on Facebook at http://www.facebook.com/antiquetrader)

- 5 percent of online consumers are active followers ("Followers" in the report) of a brand; one out of every six accounts followed on Twitter is a brand. (For an example, find *Antique Trader* on Twitter at http://twitter.com/antiquetrader) And now for the statistic that ties all of the above together: 50 percent of all online consumers have made a purchase as a result of email. The pattern is clear: Recruit fans and followers on Facebook and Twitter, but don't try to sell them anything on the social sites. Instead, engage them by offering them useful information or entertainment and let them get to know you. When they know you and like you, they will become a follower of your business. When a user "follows" your business, it is an invitation for you to interact with them. Through interaction, they will learn to trust you and your opinions, and, by extension, your products. Let the consumer approach you first. Save the selling for email, because once they have agreed that you can email them (permission-based marketing), there is a good chance that eventually they will respond to one of your offers and buy something from you.

Three steps to an effective social marketing strategy

1. Use each tool properly.

Users log on to social media sites with certain expectations. On Facebook, their expectation is to socialize with their friends and be entertained. So, offer them entertainment. Take photos of unusual items and tell a story about how it was used "back in the day." Make a video of the same item; post it on YouTube and link to it on Facebook. Facebook users love videos, and they will link to them and post them for their friends to see. Develop a reputation for posting curiosities, and you will soon have a loyal following.

On Twitter, users expect access: access to celebrities, news, and brands. You have just 140 characters to work with on Twitter, so you have to get right to the point. Post a link to your YouTube videos or an interesting picture, or offer a special deal like a free valuation. Ask a question and get their input. Interaction is the key to success on Twitter.

2. Develop a mailing list.

Consumers will give you their email addresses; you just have to give something in return. Exact Target's research listed 12 reasons why consumers would give out their email addresses; among them are:
- 67 percent in order to get discounts and promotions
- 55 percent to get a "freebie" in return for their address
- 50 percent to get product updates
- 33 percent to get access to exclusive content

3. Use your list to drive traffic to your online-offline stores.

Your mailing list will be filled with followers who have learned to know you, like you and trust you. Know-Like-Trust is the classic formula for success in word-of-mouth marketing. You will have captured the interest of new customers through online social networking — people who have found your posts and videos to be interesting and informative. You will have educated them about your products and developed in them an interest in collecting.

You must mail to this list regularly, at least once a week. Give them something of value each time: a report on a particular collectible or a link to an interesting website.

If you want to reach a new generation of buyers, you have to send your message to the place where new buyers are listening, and approach them in the manner in which they prefer to be approached.

Don't just send advertising messages, or you will find people dropping off your list. If you can't write interesting posts, hire a freelance writer to do it for you; you can find many on freelance sites such as guru.com and elance. com. List maintenance does not have to be a time-consuming chore, either. You can subscribe to an auto responder and set your program to run automatically, or you can hire a marketing company to handle the details for you.

Modern consumers are bombarded with sales messages throughout the day; they get them on TV, radio, newspapers, the Internet, snail mail, email, on buses, taxis, and everywhere else. Everyone is clamoring for the consumer's attention. Consumers are tired of the noise and tired of being interrupted for a commercial message. The dealer who takes the time to get to know and to interact with his customers through online social networking is the dealer who will develop new markets and thrive.

How to Get Search Engines to Notice Your Antiques Inventory Descriptions

Earlier in 2012, Google revised its search-results ranking algorithm in a way that will help some online sellers and hurt others. Google constantly makes "corrective" adjustments to its algorithm, in an attempt to provide better search results for users and quash those webmasters who try to "game" the system in order to gain page position.

In Google's sights this time were "content farms," sites that publish low-quality or duplicate content that is intended to drive advertising revenue rather than provide valuable content to users.

An unintended consequence of the change was that many e-stores found their page ranks drop significantly. Retailers who copied and pasted the product descriptions that were provided by their product manufacturers suffered the largest drops. Why? Because the reused descriptions were duplicate content, and all duplicate content was downgraded by Google.

Online sellers whose page positions are lowered can suffer significant drops in revenue. Conversely, sellers whose positions substantially improve may see their cash flow turn into a cash flood. America Online statistics show that on page one of search results, position No. 1 garners 42 percent of all clicks. Position No. 2 drops more than 300 percent, down to less than 12 percent of all clicks. Lowly position No. 10 receives only 3 percent of all clicks. Dealers whose products are not showing up on page 1 of Google for their keywords won't get much search traffic at all.

If Google considers product descriptions to be "online content" and rewards good content with improved page position, doesn't it make sense to spend some time "juicing up" your product descriptions? Dealers who take the time to write good descriptions — or even slightly better descriptions — may find that their page ranks improve significantly. The improvement will come not due to great writing skills but because few dealers in the antique community take the time to write compelling product descriptions.

Most antiques and auction sites display photos of their inventory items along with a physical description of the item: what it is, what it's made of, who made it, the condition, dimensions, etc. For dealers with thousands of online items, this is all the information that they have time to provide. What too many dealers overlook is that although it is the photos that engage the customer, it is the words that determine (among other things) their site's page position with the search engines. Without good page position, no one will see the photos anyway.

Good written descriptions satisfy more than just Google's search algorithm, though. The research team Lightner and Eastman at the University of South Carolina recently completed a study titled "User Preference for Product Information in Remote Purchase Environments." The study addressed the question of whether photos or words were more effective online selling devices. The results of the experiment consistently showed that written product descriptions resulted in higher levels of user satisfaction than pictures, although subjects expressed a strong preference for both words and pictures.

Successful online merchants will tell you that product descriptions are not about "show and tell," they are about "show and sell." A good description provides the shopper with item details plus the motivation to buy the item; it will engage, inform and give the shopper a reason to click the "buy now" button. In the online world, a competitor is always just a click away. It's hard enough for a merchant to develop site traffic. If one is lucky enough (or smart enough) to have site traffic, then give visitors a reason to buy while they're there. Give them more than just a photo and product dimensions; engage them and sell them.

With this in mind, allow me to offer four tips on how to improve your product descriptions:

1. Know your customer. Who will search for this item? Why do they want it? What are the points of connoisseurship for the item that will trigger a buying response in shoppers who collect this item? Don't list just the item's features; tell shoppers how a particular feature will fulfill their requirements as

a collector or satisfy them in some other way. It's the old Dale Carnegie sales formula: Never state a feature without following it with a benefit.

2. Make details come alive, and appeal to the senses. As much as possible, give your shopper the experience they would have if they examined the item in your shop. Give them what they can't see by simply looking at the photo. Describe the item's "vital statistics" in a way that helps shoppers visualize its proportions and/or function. How heavy is it? Is it smooth or rough to the touch? Is it "pocket-sized"? What emotion does the item elicit?

3. Use testimonials. Not sometimes — always. Research from the marketing company Econsultancy states that 90 percent of online consumers trust recommendations from people they know, and 70 percent of consumers trust the opinions of unknown users. If you haven't done so already, collect customer testimonials of your reliability for online sales, how much your customers like your service, how accessible you are, how friendly you are, how much the customer liked the product purchased from you, or how fast your shipping was. Use at least one testimonial on each page of your website. Your shoppers will get to know you through what others say about you.

4. Research your competitors. I'm not suggesting that you steal your competitor's product descriptions. Rather, search for products similar to yours and see what comes up on Page One of a Google search. Click on the link for the page that has the No. 1 position, and when the page appears (if you're using a PC), then right-click your mouse. When the menu comes up, select "view page source." The page that will appear contains the coding for the page you were viewing. On the page, find the lines that contain the keywords for the page. These are the keywords that helped the No. 1 page attain first position with Google. Use these keywords when you write your product description; they work.

Good product descriptions must satisfy two masters: the Google algorithm and the customer.

Ultimately, it is the customer that must be satisfied, but unless an online merchant gives Google what it is looking for, no customers will arrive to shop.

How Using Google Places Can Get Your Antiques Business Listed in Local Internet Searches

"I've never been lost," said Daniel Boone. "But I was once perplexed for a few days." It's said that Boone was a master at staying found. Making his way through the wilderness with nothing more than an incomplete map, a compass, and his own sensibilities, he blazed a trail that thousands would follow from Virginia to Kentucky.

"Staying found" is a significant challenge for brick-and-mortar antiques stores. New customers will stumble upon stores that are located on well-traveled thoroughfares. Dealers who pump money into traditional media advertising (newspapers, radio, yellow pages) may also attract new customers. But high-traffic locations and traditional media advertising are very expensive, and many dealers simply can't justify such high overhead. So, they hope that new customers will find them through word-of-mouth rather than a proactive promotional campaign.

Before you turn the page, let me tell you that this isn't going to be another spiel about the virtues of inexpensive Internet advertising. You should already know that your business needs a website, and that the website has to have good content, targeted keywords, and be search-engine optimized. However, you can have all that and still be lost in the wilderness of Google or Bing search results.

If your website is lost in the wilderness, Google Places can significantly increase your chances of being found, and it's free. It will take you about 15 minutes to get it set up, and another couple of hours to optimize your listing. If you're already on Google Places, I'll tell you a simple trick to optimize your listing and improve your chance of moving up in the Google page ranking.

For those who are not familiar with Google Places, it is an online business listing that produces targeted local results whenever searchers search by keyword and geographic location. Returned search results include a map with pushpin graphics that are coded to match the search results and show the geographic location of the business.

When a geographic location is included in the search inquiry, Google will always list the "Google Places" results at the top of the search results. If your website has been languishing on page four or five (or worse) of search results in your area, Google Places will move you forward in the results.

However, even though you may be moved up in line, remember that sometimes it can be a very long line. A search of "antiques Washington DC" returned more than 13 million Google results (note these are results; not the number of stores!), and the first 15 pages were all Google Places business listings. Even in this exclusive group, your business can still get lost in the wilderness.

The keyword "antiques" has a lot of competition; it's a very broad term. If you want more customers to find you via the Internet, you'll need to be more specific with your keywords, and tie them in to Google Places. For example, let's say that one of my shop's profit centers is antique lighting. When I'm filling out the listing form in Google Places, I'd list "antique lighting" as one of my categories. That way, I stand a better chance of being found.

To really focus on your keywords, use Google's Keyword Tool to choose keywords with the highest number of actual searches and the lowest amount of competition.

Step by step, here's how to get more customers for free by maximizing your Google Places listing:

If you haven't already, sign up for a Google Places account.

Before filling out the GP form, correlate your profit centers with high-volume, low competition keywords using the Google Keyword Tool (link above) and use those keywords as your categories. It's to your advantage to use keywords that searchers are actually using.

Do some random searches on your products, competition, and city.

Take note of antiques and related businesses (art, framing, restoration, etc.) that consistently get high page position in your searches.

Glean the keywords of the top websites in your desired categories. Their keywords were a factor in getting them top page position, and there's no legal or ethical reason that you can't use them as well. Here's how to find out what they are:

a. Go to the home page of site you're interested in.

b. Right-click anywhere on the page; when the menu comes up, choose "View Page Source."

c. The page that comes up will be the under-the-hood coding for the page you are viewing.

-Look for the line that says "keywords." Following that will be their keywords; find ones that apply to your site.

-In the Google search bar, enter each keyword that you intend to use.

-When the results display, go to each website listed in the Google Places results and view the businesses review page.

-At the bottom of the review page, you will see a link that says something like "reviews from around the web." These domains are where Google is pulling the information to rate and review the business. More quality links equals better rank. Many of these sources are open directories and review sites where you can list your business. Use as many of them as you can to build links back to your Google Places listing.

It's critical that when you list your business with these directories that each listing perfectly matches the information in your Google Places listing. The Google Maps algorithm relies not only on the number of links back to your listing, but the quality and consistency of those sources. So, if your listing address is "161 West Street Annapolis MD 21401," don't use "161 West St. Annapolis Maryland 21401" in the review directories. Every listing must match exactly so that the search bots see them as the same address.

If you want your business to "stay found," local search is the bandwagon that you need to be on.

If Daniel Boone's wilderness had changed as often as the Google landscape, he might never have made it through the Cumberland Gap and back. For Boone, at least, landmarks stayed put. Not so with Google. They update their ranking algorithm once or twice a year, and every time they do they throw the online world into a tizzy. For now, Google seems to be moving in the direction of improved local search. If you want your business to "stay found," local search is the bandwagon that you need to be on.

How Antiques and Vintage Dealers Can Use Facebook to Build Trust Without Alienating Customers

Walking down Main Street in Mt. Airy, N.C., I feel like I've stepped into a 1960s sitcom. Mt. Airy, the boyhood home of Andy Griffith, was the inspiration for his television hometown of Mayberry. As I stroll by Floyd's Barber Shop, I peek inside and notice that all the chairs are full. Not the barber chairs, but the waiting chairs against the wall. Those seated are engaged in animated conversation, and a crowd has gathered to listen to the dialogue.

This is a common sight here in the Blue Ridge Mountains. Residents gathered in a local store to visit and gossip. Sociologists call such gathering spots a "Third Place." A Third Place is a social venue, which is separate from home and work that fosters broader communication between participants and builds a sense of belonging and community.

In his 1989 book, *The Great Good Place*, author Ray Oldenburg asserts that a good Third Place is accessible, comfortable, nearby, involves regulars, and is open to both new and old friends.

Sounds like Facebook to me.

Facebook's growth has been explosive, and it's no wonder. Social meeting places are vital to all communities. Americans lead too-busy lives. We spend more time at work than citizens of other developed countries, take fewer vacations, and try to cram every minute of "family time" with sports teams, scouts, karate lessons, music lessons, swimming lessons — well, you get the picture. Facebook is as near as our computer, open to new and old friends, and we don't have to leave the comfort of our home to participate. It's an ideal Third Place.

Absent from the description of a Third Place is "exchanging advertising messages." Imagine that you're with a group that's chatting at Floyd's Barber Shop when a man walks in interrupts your conversation, hands you a business card that says "Insurance R Us" and attempts to sell you life insurance. Would you stay to listen or would you politely excuse yourself? How about your friends? You probably wouldn't stay. Commercial activity, when done to excess, spoils a Third Place. No one likes it, and participants develop an aversion to the offending member.

Yet, the above scenario is repeated regularly on Facebook. Marketing gurus everywhere insist that businesses MUST get involved in social media marketing. Many business owners hear the word "marketing" but not the word "social." So, they slap up a Facebook fan page, fanatically market their wares, and soon discover that that they aren't driving traffic to their websites or getting new customers. The reason is that they've alienated their readers.

Many business owners hear the word "marketing" but not the word "social."

Winston Churchill aptly described such attempts at social marketing when he said, "A fanatic is one who can't change his mind and won't change the subject."

Facebook is not an eBay store; it's a Third Place.

"That's why they call it social media," says Leslie Coty, Social Media Strategist and President of Coty Connections. "Social Media is a game-changer; it's changed the way we communicate, and it's changed the way that we do business." Coty should know about the "changing game." She spent more than two decades in traditional media sales: print, radio, and television. "The marketplace has become overcrowded with competing advertising messages," she says. "Consumers have developed a resistance to traditional advertising, and sales messages aren't getting through."

What consumers want, according to Coty, is to trust the person from whom they are buying things. Trust implies a relationship; consumers want to buy from people, not faceless corporations. Where corporations are involved in commercial transactions, consumers want to deal face-to-face with someone they have built a relationship with. Relationships are built one at a time, not mass-produced.

How then, can an antiques dealer use social media to build relationships with new customers? Coty offers dealers five tips on how this can be accomplished:

Become a follower. Read other's posts and join in the conversation. Stay on-topic, and avoid controversy. As threads develop, you'll learn the names of people who actively participate in conversational threads. Friend them, and then participate in their conversations. Your network of friends and potential customers will grow.

Provide content that your friends will want to read and then forward to other friends. Be a source of expert information and/or entertainment for your friends. Post links to articles that you found interesting or videos that you found funny. Your friends will come to value your expertise and your friendship, and as they learn to trust you they will approach you for advice.

Link your website to your Facebook page. Put a Facebook "Like" icon (or something similar) on your website, and post links to your website from your Facebook page.

Limit product links from Facebook to your website; no more than 15 percent of your posts should be product-related.

Use Facebook ads. Facebook can target an audience better than traditional media ever could. Advertisers can target by age, interests, location, education, connections, and more. Would you like your ad to appear on the home page of 30-somethings who live in your city, and have an interest in model trains? Facebook can do that.

I'd like to add two more items to Coty's list:

Use the new Facebook "Questions" application. Gather customer intelligence and then use that information to help determine what you will post on your page. (The "Questions" application is the one in which your friends respond to a poll, and the results are posted in a bar graph). For example, suppose you posted the question "What do you enjoy collecting the most?" and you listed three possible responses: furniture, glassware, or memorabilia. If you found that the largest percentage of your friends favored collecting memorabilia, you could increase your readership by posting more "memorabilia" links.

Be genuine. Don't think for a minute that you can fake sincerity over the long haul. If you fake sincerity for economic gain, you're a conman, not a merchant.

If there's a key to social media marketing, it's this: Relationships are first, selling is second.

How eBay's Fraud Protection Plan Boosts Your Sales (Even if You Don't Sell on eBay)

Bay fraud appeared in the news again with the 2011 headline, "Three eBay Fraud Rings Dismantled in Romania." Romania must be a hotbed of Internet-scam artistry. Just a few years before, a headline read, "Small Romanian Town Gets Rich Through eBay Scams."

In the 2011 scam, ads were posted on eBay and Craigslist offering a variety of merchandise, ranging from cars to electronics. Internet users were defrauded of about $20 million. The busts were a coup for the Romanian National Police and the FBI, who made about 90 arrests in 117 raids on nine towns.

Now, forgive my obtuseness, but I can't find anywhere in the article where it says that eBay scammed anybody. So, why does the headline declare "eBay Fraud?" The words "eBay" "eBay Fraud" and "eBay Scam" appear so often in the media that one would think that eBay is used only by con artists and the feeble minded.

Apparently, the nearly 3 million successful daily transactions completed via eBay fail to be the stuff of headlines. In spite of the alleged $20 million per year that eBay spends on fraud protection, consumers in search of "something for nothing" continue to get scammed by con-artists looking to make a quick buck. I guess Forrest Gump's mama was right: "Stupid is as stupid does."

Such scams are not new. They simply are more accessible to average citizens who get a little greedy. The arrests in Romania are just another chapter in the ongoing saga of Internet fraud. Scams like these make headlines, and headlines sell newspapers, magazines and web traffic.

Of course, fraud exists wherever there is opportunity and greed, and there always have been plenty of both in the art and antiques businesses. The public perception is that art and antiques are "valuable," but average consumers don't have the tools or expertise to properly evaluate either. Hence, they are easy prey for con artists.

Fuzzy photos and misleading descriptions offered by some online sellers make proper evaluation risky, if not impossible. Items that were sold yesterday as "guaranteed to pass expert scrutiny" are discovered to be fakes by today's technology.

Reputable dealers will own up to past mistakes. Delaware's Winterthur Museum, a former DuPont estate that specializes in early American paintings and decorative art, recently came clean about some of the fakes in its exhibits. In a collection of more than 1,000 silver pieces attributed to Paul Revere and his contemporaries, more than 75 percent were found to be early 20th century fakes meant to deceive collectors.

The distrust of eBay as a marketplace has spread like a virus and infected all online sellers, including you and me.

Winterthur scientists also exposed forgeries of George Washington letters, portraits by Charles Wilson Peale and a Thomas Jefferson desk. The DuPont family relied on their curators and archaeologists, but if they were fooled, the rest of us are certainly disadvantaged.

Fast-forward from the early 20th century to the early 21st century, and forgery is a thriving Internet business. No longer the exclusive purview of one-man shops, antiques and antiquities forgery have become cottage industries accessible to anyone with a creative flair and an Internet service provider. Using local materials often acquired from archaeological sites, small manufacturers in Peru, Bolivia, and elsewhere are making remarkably accurate copies of actual artifacts. Selling these "artifacts" on eBay is more profitable than digging around in ruins for days and then passing their finds through a long line of middlemen.

Repeated headlines and forum posts exposing online scams and frauds create an atmosphere of distrust regarding eBay. Also, some users have expressed that the "feedback" system on eBay is an unreliable indicator of the trustworthiness of a buyer or seller. Most of us are reluctant to give (well-deserved) negative feedback to a buyer or seller for fear that we will get (undeserved) negative feedback in return. Having a high positive feedback rating is greatly desired by eBay buyers and sellers. Few want to risk taking any action that will negatively affect their feedback ratings.

The distrust of eBay as a marketplace has spread like a virus and infected all online sellers, including you and me. Distrust — and trust — are pervasive ideas. Annually, the Edelman Trust Barometer measures the public's trust of businesses, governments, and countries worldwide. Edelman also measures the economic cost of mistrust (a "trust tax") and trust (a "trust dividend"). No specific barometers are given for the antiques trade or online selling, but there is a clear corollary between trust and consumer response.

When your business is trusted, 51 percent of consumers will believe positive information about you after hearing it only one or two times, but only 25 percent will believe negative information about you. When your business is not trusted, 57 percent of consumers will believe negative information about you after hearing it just once or twice, and only 15 percent will believe positive information about you.

There is a direct relationship between trust and your bottom line. Risk is one determinate of price; high risk lowers prices, and low risk raises prices. Lack of trust implies higher risk, and higher risk equates to lower prices for all online sellers. In the words of Columbia Business School professor John Whitney: "Mistrust doubles the cost of doing business."

John F. Kennedy said, "A rising tide lifts all boats." The reverse is also true: An ebb tide lowers all boats. Surely we, as antiques dealers, are all in the same boat. We all contribute to the public perception of the trustworthiness of online buying and selling. When a giant like eBay is associated with scams and frauds, it hurts all of us.

eBay's Fraud Protection Program is a response to the atmosphere of distrust. Without trust, a loyal user base cannot be established, and without loyal customers a company cannot grow.

Let's give credit to eBay for making an effort to sort all of this out. Its efforts to control fraud help all of us as online sellers.

Video Marketing for Antiques Dealers:

If You Can Take a Digital Photo, Then You Can Create a Low-Cost Digital Commercial

The Super Bowl attracted over 111 million viewers in 2012. The $3-million-for-30-seconds price tag breaks down to less than 3 cents per viewer. Not bad for a cost-per-impression.

But hold on to your seats: 111 million viewers a year is a drop in the bucket compared to how many viewers YouTube is pulling in every month. According to a recent study by comScore, 147 million viewers watched 14 billion videos on YouTube in the month of May 2011. Add in the other video hosting sites, and the total views for online video was almost 34 million in May 2010. That's like having a Super-Bowl-sized audience every day, and the Internet delivers that many viewers 24/7, all year. Even in prime time, NBC, CBS, Fox, CNN, and all the television networks combined don't reach that viewership level.

You can reach these viewers, and it won't cost you $3 million to do so. Know what it costs to put a video up on YouTube? Nothing. Zip. Nada. And, you can make a video for next to nothing. The video creation site that I use charges $30 per year for unlimited videos. I can make a nice video in roughly half an hour using still photographs. Remember, the primary purpose of video is to drive traffic to your website or store, not to sell your item from the video.

When videos are properly tagged and titled, they can show up on the first page of Google in about a day. With proper optimization, a video is 53 times more likely than static content to show up on the first page of Google (Forrester, January 2010). So, you can access a massive audience for pennies a day. Or, you can opt for advertising on the Super Bowl. You choose.

Do you still have reservations about moving into video marketing? Consider three more statistics (I promise I'll then lay off the statistics):

- Reckitt Benckiser, a consumer packaged goods firm, found that online video delivered a 6 percent increase in their in-store sales (Reckitt Benckiser / Nielsen, May 2010).

- Internet Retailer reports that visitors who view product videos are 85 percent more likely to buy than visitors who do not (Internet Retailer, April 2010).

- Video in email marketing has been shown to increase click-through rates by over 96 percent. (Implix 2010 Email Marketing Trends Survey).

Five ideas to get you started with your first video

-Take still photos of your shop, employees and key inventory items and turn them into a video.

-Make a series of videos on "points of connoisseurship" for selected inventory items.

-Arrange with a local auctioneer to take photos or a video of auction highlights, and share the credit with the auctioneer.

-Create your own version of *American Pickers* and shoot some video as you go yard sale shopping.

-Shoot video at antique shows, fairs, or other large events.

The important concept is to start getting your videos online. It won't be long before all your competitors will be doing this, and if you want to build a following you should be an early adopter. Once you have a dozen or so videos you can create your own YouTube channel and build a subscriber list.

If you'd like to script a sales message to promote your shop you will only need six to eight photos with text slides in-between, for a total of 15 slides. Video speeds are adjustable, but in general 15 slides moving within the pre-formatted graphics display will result in a 1-minute 30-second "commercial" for your shop.

With proper optimization, a video is 53 times more likely than static content to show up on the first page of Google

Scripting is easy if you follow this format for your text slides; just answer these questions, and your answers become the slide text. Keep the answers short.

What is your target looking for? Hint: It's not "the best antique shop." It's a fun afternoon of shopping, or recalling their youth, or some other benefit.

Considering the first answer, what will the customer actually find at your shop?

What's the No. 1 benefit of shopping in your store?

What's the No. 2 benefit of shopping at your store?

What's the "emotional hook" for the customer? What sort of satisfaction will they receive from shopping in your store?

What's the decision you want them to make? Here's where you put your "call to action."

Predict the future: "They'll be glad they came" or "They'll find the perfect gift" or whatever fulfills the promises made in your presentation.

Be sure to list your contact information in the final text slide, and maybe a Google Map of your location (see AntiqueTrader.com for instructions on how to create a Google Map for your shop).

When you tag and title your project, use keywords so that Google can find and index the video. Keywords are the words that searchers type into the Google search bar when they're looking for something. If your title reflects what consumers are typing, then Google will know that your video matches the consumer's interest and will bring back your video in the search results. You can target the number of consumers that enter a particular keyword by using the Google Keyword Tool.

For example, a recent search of the keyword tool showed that the phrase "antique jewelry" had 74,000 specific searches in one month, whereas the phrase "antiques and collectables" only had only 9,900 specific searches. If your shop carries antique jewelry, choosing the former over the latter will give you a potentially larger audience.

Here are four video creation sites that can process your videos; most of them have simple drag-and-drop features that enable you to make a video without any special equipment or expertise. Some have the capability to add music and text, and provide direct upload links to YouTube. I personally use Animoto and Google Search Stories. Both are easy to use.

http://animoto.com/sample-videos

http://www.onetruemedia.com/

http://www.stupeflix.com/

https://searchstories-intl.appspot.com/en-us/

You may not become the Martin Scorsese of antiques videos, and it's unlikely that your videos will attract Super-Bowl-sized audiences. But your mailing list will grow, and you will become somewhat of a local celebrity.

More importantly, your shop and your offerings will be prominently displayed on Google, Bing and Yahoo – that's got to be good for business.

Top Antiques Apps for Your iPad or Android Tablet

Pricing antiques? There's an app for that but an overall lack of apps leaves room for innovation

We live in an age of specialists. In almost every profession, the amount of information available is too overwhelming to be mastered by one individual. Doctors, lawyers, real estate agents, and personal property appraisers — individuals in too many professions to count — are specialists, not generalists. The day of the generalist is over.

Even technology is trending toward specialization. Soon to be gone are big, multi-function software programs. It used to be that big, multi-function programs offered a great value. For a modest price, you could buy the Swiss Army Knife of software that included a word processor, database, spreadsheet, customer relationship management and more. But with each new version of the software came new features, and soon such software became a victim of its own size.

Eventually, every big program reaches a point where there are so many features offered that access to them becomes difficult and makes the whole product impractical for the average user. How big would a Swiss Army Knife have to be before it became unusable? If the knife had 50 tools, how many would you actually use? Would you rather pay a hefty price for a knife full of tools that you didn't use, or would you rather have a useful, practical knife at a modest — or nonexistent — price?

Useful and practical is the trend in software applications, and nowhere is that trend more apparent than in mobile applications for iPad, Android, and other smart devices. In 2011, there were more than 17 billion mobile application downloads and this number is predicted to reach 100 billion downloads by 2014. Not all of these are free downloads, either: 20 percent of the downloads were purchased. Consumers prefer applications that are straightforward and purpose-oriented.

Mobile apps are straightforward, single-purpose applications that move us away from a generic browser-based view of the Internet into a customized, 24/7 world of information that is obtained and organized specifically for a particular user. Plus, they have the added benefit of being "on" all the time; you don't have to be plugged in to your DSL, cable or satellite connection to gain access.

Don't confuse mobile applications with old-school mobile device access to a website. Using a mobile device, consumers can reach any website that has been configured for mobile access. Typically, such access is limited and difficult to manage; visualize trying to squeeze a 15-inch desktop computer screen down into the 3 or 4-inch screen of a smartphone. Get the picture? There's a lot of scrolling involved. Mobile applications, on the other hand, are specifically designed to work on a particular device platform and are

Useful and practical is the trend in software applications, in mobile applications for iPad, Android, and other smart devices.

configured to provide full access to a company's available data. How do you recognize which is which? Mobile applications must be downloaded. If the website/membership you are looking at doesn't require that an application be downloaded, then you probably won't have full access to their information from your mobile device.

There are many mobile applications available for antique dealers and collectors. In fact, there are way too many to cover here. If you're interested in an in-depth look at what's available, just Google "apps for antique dealers" or "apps for collectors" and you'll have plenty of reading.

Before you search for apps that will serve you well in your hobby or business, there are a few things you need to know:

Not all apps are available for all mobile platforms. If you find exactly what you're looking for at the iPad store but you own an Android, keep looking or buy another device. In fact, as of this writing I could find no worthwhile antiques-related mobile applications for Android. Yes, there are applications available but I found them to be redundant and not much more than ebooks or personal-collection databases. There is hope for Android users, though: I understand that there are several antiques applications in development by reputable companies. More on that as the situation develops.

Most apps have a notoriously short life. According to a recent study by Pinch Media, 30 percent of mobile users discard iPhone apps the day after buying and downloading them from Apple's App Store. As you can imagine, the throw-away rate is even higher for free apps, with about 80 percent of users discarding them the day after download. After 30 days, fewer than 5 percent of downloaded apps are still being used. Before you click the "download" link, know the limitations of the application. Stick with applications from large, well-known companies, because the failure rate of small-time app developers is extremely high. If you're not familiar with the company, understand that their app may not be around next week.

There's a lot of duplication in available apps. For example, there are several apps on the market that will provide directions to your (or someone else's) store. This is such a simple function that many larger apps include it as a feature. When choosing an app, ask yourself what functionality you expect, and search for a product that will give you what you want in one product. If you can get product search, geo-locator, pricing, photos and points of connoisseurship from just one application, then information will be much easier to access than if you had to open up four applications to accomplish the same end.

Here are two apps that have proven themselves useful in the antiques marketplace for price research, locating products and marketing. They are the only ones that I can recommend at this time.

Worthpoint Mobile Application: This application gives dealers and collectors the ability to access Worthpoint's database of 120 million-plus records and images from online marketplaces and auction houses. The data available covers a wide range of items including stamps, coins, fine art, sports memorabilia and access to the latest information, articles and news in the antique/collectible industry. Also provided is a geo-locator that identifies antique stores within a specified geographic range. The app is available for iPad and iPhone and the download is free, but you must have a Worthpoint membership to access the database. The app is a standard feature for all three Worthpoint subscription plans. Worthpoint spokesperson Britni Zandbergen confirms that as of June 9, the Worthpoint application has had more than 22,300 downloads. Clearly, dealers and collectors are finding the Worthpoint application useful. You can download the app from http://www.worthpoint.com/about/mobile.

eBay Mobile Application: If you're an active eBay seller and own an iPad or iPhone, then you should have this app … because it's free. It's also a very useful tool for eBay traders, because all the selling and listing functions that are available on your desktop computer are available to your mobile device. Plus, you have the added benefits of a barcode scanner that enables you to research items and import the details right into your listing, and you can access PayPal right from your phone. You can download the app from http://mobile.ebay.com.

Antiques dealers spend a lot of time on the road. Those who have an iPhone or iPad and a useful mobile application have a distinct advantage over dealers whose only online access is their desktop computer. The right app is more than a piece of software; it's a 24/7 personal assistant. It's a dog that always brings you your slippers. It's a big lever that can move your business. With such an app, you can have a specialist's knowledge right at your fingertips.

Why Half of Your New Customers Can't Find Your Antiques Retail Website: It's Not Showing Up on Their Smartphones

What three things do you always take with you when you leave your house? Almost universally, the answer is your keys, your wallet, and your phone. For decades, urban dwellers left home with just their keys and their wallets. At some point, cell phones became so important that they couldn't leave home without them, either.

A few years ago, high-tech guru George Forrester said, "If you look at the history of technology, there is a threshold where one day, you had to have something. You had to have a fax machine. Remember that day? It was 1981 or something. You had to have a fax machine on that day. The day before, you didn't need it."

When did you decide that you absolutely had to have a cell phone? I grudgingly got mine when a big client insisted that I be available by phone while I was on the road. That was about 1998. Within weeks, I was hooked. I never left home without it.

The rate at which new technologies are being adopted by our society as a whole is phenomenal. It took 15 years for radio to be adopted by 80 percent of American homes. It took 10 years for television to reach the same penetration. Telephones didn't reach 80 percent penetration until the early 1960s — almost 50 years from the time that they were introduced. Cell phones, which became commonplace about 15 years ago, are now almost universal but are being replaced by smartphones. Just three years ago, smartphone penetration stood at 21 percent in the U.S. In 2011, it exceeded 50 percent.

It's predicted that within two years, smartphones will reach 90 percent market penetration in the U.S. Clearly, Americans have decided it's time to get smartphones.

Consumers with smartphones have affected the economy at almost every level. Why? Because when folks are out shopping, looking for a place to eat or looking for something to do (like shop for antiques), they turn to their smartphones to find out who's around that can meet their needs. It might be your business; it might not.

Consider this: Right now, one half of local searches are done on a mobile device (smartphone). Half of all customers looking for an antiques shop are doing so on their phones. Do you think this number is likely to go up, or down? If your website isn't mobile compatible, then those prospects can't find you. As far as new customers are concerned,

Now is the time for your business to go mobile. The paradigm shift in the way that people communicate and do business is real. And it's happening now.

you don't exist. You are losing half of your potential customers to your competitor (provided he has a mobile-ready website). How long can you continue to lose half of your prospects before you are out of business altogether?

A friend recently related this story: He and his wife were on the interstate at dinnertime, and they wanted Chinese food. They typed "Chinese food (city)" into their Android phone, and the search results indicated that the closest Chinese restaurant was about 20 miles off their driving route. They settled for fast food, because there was a hamburger place at their exit. When they had eaten and continued their journey, they discovered that there was a Chinese restaurant at the very next highway exit. It was a missed meal for them and a missed customer for the Chinese restaurant. The restaurant didn't show up in search results because the restaurant wasn't indexed in Google's mobile website index.

There's no longer any question that the web is going mobile. Big companies already know this. They did the research and have invested their money where they know they will get a return.

In 2009 alone, consumers purchased $1.6 billion worth of products through their mobile phones. That's right, $1.6 billion. That's a lot, and that's reason enough that three out of four companies are expected to invest in mobile marketing this year.

Technology has moved on, and your business must move on with it. You can't stand still. It's time once again to revamp your web presence to adapt to the mobile Internet. It's a shame, really. You probably spent a lot of money getting your existing website up and running and looking good. You spent even more money keeping the content current.

But imagine cramming that big web page down into the size of your smart-phone. That's a 3.5-inch screen. Your laptop is at least four times bigger. How much scrolling would you have to do (up, down, right and left) to read the information on a standard web page? Quite a bit. If you arrived at a website where you were forced to scroll at the end of every line, how long would you stay on that page? Not very long, I suspect.

How long do you think your customers will look at your website on their mobile devices? If your site hasn't been configured for mobile devices, they won't look for very long. Neither would you.

Have you looked at your site on your mobile phone? Maybe you should. Of course, since there are so many makes and models of phones, it's impossible to see what your site looks like on all of them unless you use a mobile phone emulator. There are a variety of emulators online that can mimic how your site looks on various mobile devices.

Have a look at your site on various phones; you'll be surprised at what you find.

Now is the time for your business to go mobile, and here are several compelling reasons:

The barriers to entry are low; the desirable dot-mobi URLs for local businesses are still available in most business categories.

Mobile marketing is affordable. The cost to have your website optimized for mobile is considerably less than the cost of building your site the first time around.

You have advertising options you didn't have with your "regular" website. Sending opt-in advertising text messages to your customers is cheaper than any other form of direct advertising, except for email.

It's easy to track your advertising results. You'll know how many customers looked at your offer and exactly when they looked at it. Can you say that about newspaper, yellow pages or radio advertising?

I know what you're thinking: It seems like there's always some big new thing available. And people say that if you don't get the big new thing, then you're in danger of losing customers and going out of business. You've probably heard it all before. And I have to admit that sometimes, you don't always need the latest gadget.

But I'm not talking about getting the latest gadget. I'm talking about a sea change or paradigm shift in the way that people communicate and do business. This is real. This is happening now.

Sixty years ago, your decision would have been whether to keep using the telegraph to do business or to upgrade to one of those newfangled telephones. Now, you have to decide whether you're going to go mobile or not. It's the same decision. Only the technology has changed.

And if you don't believe it's that serious, just ask the Western Union Telegraph Co. They'll be happy to explain it to you.

Three Ways Google Insights for Search Will Improve Your Antiques Business

E veryone wants to know what's hot, what's selling, and what's not. Fashion, entertainment, shopping, news, and technology all have their daily "trending now" web updates.

Every day, someone, somewhere, publishes another "Top 10" list, but when it comes to providing actionable information for running your business, most are about as useful as David Letterman's laugh-filled Top 10.

"What's Hot" lists are not uncommon in the antiques trade, but since there is no standardized reporting format (like there is in larger industries), it's difficult to interpret the list results in terms of an individual dealer's local market. To be effective, a "What's Hot" list would have to be assembled for each market. If you knew that consumers were looking for an item that you regularly inventoried, you could almost certainly get a return on some quick advertising or start carrying items people really want.

Fortunately, dealers can assemble an effective "hot list" using tools freely available on the Internet — the same tools used by web publishers to assemble their "trending now" lists. There is one tool that is particularly useful, and if you learn how to use it, you will be pleased and surprised by the insights it can give you into your market: Google Insights for Search.

Google Insights for Search is an offshoot of Google Trends. Google Trends shows search-term use over a period of time. Insights is like Trends on steroids: In addition to search-term usage over time, you can search volume patterns across geographic regions, multiple categories and even images or news items.

Here are three ways that you can use Insights to improve your antiques business:

1. Focus your advertising message. The No. 1 rule in both print and on-line advertising is to first get the prospect's attention. Whether you're talking about a search engine's "spider bot" or an individual, using the right word can make the difference between being seen and being missed. Let's say that you're a collectibles dealer and you're about to run a print ad for your baseball collectibles; your ad will feature Topps baseball cards. In your ad, do you call them "baseball cards," "trading cards," "sports cards" or "Topps cards"? Does it make a difference what they are called? It certainly does. Let's look at an example using Insights.

On the search page enter these four card terms and then set the filters to show data from the U.S. as a whole (U.S./All sub-regions/All metros) and adjust the time period to show results from the past 12 months. What you'll find (as of this writing) is that the top term is clearly "sports cards" followed by "baseball cards" and "trading cards," with "Topps cards" a distant fourth. If you had advertised "Topps cards," your online ad would have pulled poorly, and your print ad might not have fared any better.

Dealers can assemble an effective "hot list" using tools freely available on the Internet — the same tools used by web publishers to assemble their powerful "trending now" lists.

Now let's focus on a couple of local markets, looking for the same information. We find that in the New Jersey suburbs of New York City, the terms "baseball cards" and "sports cards" are in a dead heat for searches. "Topps cards" gets no results whatsoever. But if we stay in New Jersey and change the location to the Philadelphia suburbs, "sports cards" edges out "baseball cards" and "trading cards" and "Topps cards" again get no results.

Why the difference in results? Because people in different locations use different words to refer to the same object.

2. Predict seasonal interest. Let's stick with our term "sports cards" but change the "Compare by" field from "Search Terms" to "Time Ranges." In a search for results from 2004 to present, we see right away that there has been a steady downward trend in searches for sports cards over the past eight years. In examining the graph, we see that searches for sports cards peak twice every year: at Christmas (no surprise) and in late summer. I'm not a sports cards dealer, so I don't know if that's a surprise or not (after all, it is baseball season). One thing I can tell for certain by looking at the chart: If I was going to run a promotion featuring sports cards, I would do it at Christmas or in late summer when interest is at its peak, not in March or September. If you look further down the results page, you will see two "top 10" lists (there's no getting away from them, is there?). The first is a list of the top 10 states that generate sports cards searches; the second is a list of search terms related to "sports cards" and what sort of search volume it generates.

3. Examine interest based on geography. This feature works best if your search term has broad interest ("antiques" rather than "sports cards"); there has to be enough searches in an area to generate data). Change the "Compare by" menu to "Locations." Enter whatever locations you want data from, and then enter the search term you wish to investigate. For this example, I'm using New York, Virginia and Florida (all metros) and the search term "antiques" for the last 12 months. The results are not what I would have expected: Virginia generates about 50 percent more searches for "antiques" than does either New York or Florida, with most of the interest coming from the Richmond/Petersburg areas and the Washington D.C. suburbs. This is good to know if you are scouting for retail locations.

I hope I've convinced you that "what's hot" is Google Insights for Search. It's another great tool for the toolbox of forward thinking antiques dealers.

Section 4:
Practical Tips that Work

'Retail Anthropology': Traffic Flow in Antiques Shops

By arranging your store's fixtures in a fashion that directs traffic flow and keeps high-profit items in the most visible locations, you can keep customers in your store longer and increase sales.

Have you ever focused your attention on the way you walk? Do you stand straight with your shoulders back, or do you lean forward? Do you saunter or walk quickly? Have you noticed how the customers in your store walk? Most independent retailers give little thought to how their customers walk and move through their stores. These same retailers might be surprised to learn that there is a science dedicated to the study of how customers move within a retail store: it's called "retail anthropology."

Retail anthropology was developed by Paco Underhill, who runs a consulting company called Envirosell. Back in the 1970s, Paco began to videotape the way customers move within retail stores. His objective was to find ways to improve traffic flow and increase sales. In the past 40 years, he has compiled over 100,000 hours of videotape. Forty years of watching customers move through stores has led to some irrefutable conclusions about the basics of an effective store layout. Envirosell's client lists — including AT&T, Starbucks, Blockbuster, and Apple, to name a few — attest to the value of his work.

Let's have some fun by applying Underhill's observations to an imaginary antiques store (let's call it Dusty's Antiques) and see what sort of improvements we can make to the layout.

Dusty's is like many antiques stores that you've seen: The perimeter is lined with furniture, the walls are filled with artsy décor, the outdated fixtures and shelves are arranged into aisles, and every horizontal surface in the store is covered with various collectibles. Let's follow our imaginary customer (Ms. Browser) as she approaches, enters, and shops in the store.

Dusty's Antiques is located in an urban area of shops and office buildings and has sidewalk access. Ms. Browser is on her lunch break, so she is moving at a fairly fast pace down the sidewalk. She passes by the window displays of most stores because her peripheral vision can't detect the details of window displays that are laid out parallel to the window glass. Dusty, however, knows that in order for his display to catch Ms. Browser's attention, it must be laid out in an inverted "V" shape so that pedestrians walking in both directions will be able to see his display from at least 25 feet away. Dusty has included in his display a silver tea set and some antique hand mirrors. Ms. Browser slows down to have a look at the display.

Most independent retailers give little thought to how their customers walk and move through their stores.

Underhill observations:

1. People slow down for reflective surfaces. So include some bright and shiny items in your window display. Change your display when pedestrians stop slowing down to look.

2. Angle the display so that it can be seen from 25 feet away, and keep your window clean!

Ms. Browser enters the store. Dusty has his newest items on a shelf to the right of the door, but Ms. Browser doesn't see them; her eyes are adjusting to the change in light (and, by the way, what's that odor? It's a faint hint of mildew and roses; must be that new air freshener, Eau de Thriftstore). Ms. Browser notices the cash/wrap (register) area immediately on the left, so she turns right and moves into the store.

Underhill observations:

1. Customers need a "decompression zone" of 5 to 15 paces to gear down from walking speed to shopping speed and adjust to the lighting of your store. Don't put anything that you want to be seen in the decompression zone.

2. The air in your store will have a distinct odor; make sure that it is a pleasant one. If your customers notice mildew, they will be reluctant to buy. Use an air treatment system rather than masking odors with a chemical spray.

Ms. Browser moves to the far right wall and walks down the aisle, looking ahead toward the back wall. She occasionally glimpses to the right and to the left, noticing only the items that are at her eye level.

Underhill observations:

1. In America, people walk and drive to the right, a principle called the "Invariant Right." The right wall is the most valuable real estate in your store. Placing your best merchandise on the right side will pull shoppers to the back of your store.

2. People walk facing forward, and their eyes are in the front of their head. If you want your merchandise to get the most exposure, arrange your displays so that they can be seen "face-on." Place some shelves and displays at right angles to the aisle, so that shoppers can see the best merchandise without having to turn their heads to look. If you use department signage, place the signs at right angles to the traffic flow, not flat against the wall. Use end-caps on all of your aisles. Shoppers will rarely bend or stoop to look at an item. Rotate your shelved stock so that every couple of weeks your "eye level" merchandise changes; that way, your inventory will always seem fresh to your regular customers.

Ms. Browser reaches the back wall, and stops to admire a particularly beautiful, expensive music box. To the right of the expensive music box is an equally beautiful but less expensive music box, which she picks up. She lingers over the music boxes long enough to attract Dusty's attention. Dusty engages Ms. Browser in conversation, and sells her the less expensive (but more profitable) music box.

Underhill observation:

1. Most people are right-handed, so they tend to pick up items that are placed to the right of where they are standing. Dusty was wise to place his "traffic-stopper" music box at the end of an aisle and smarter still to place a high-profit item where it stood the best chance of being picked up.

Ms. Browser continues to shop along the back wall of the store, bypassing the grocery store-style aisles on her left. When she reaches the far wall, she turns left and proceeds to the cash-wrap.

Underhill observation:

1. If a main traffic lane is built into the layout of your store, most customers will unconsciously follow the lane around the store. In a small store, this might be a simple "U," starting at the door, extending along both sides of a single row of gondolas, and ending back at the cash wrap. In a larger store, this path might be a wide lane with specialty alcoves on each side. Customers can stop and shop, but when they're ready to leave, they have to get back on the path. Place the products of highest importance in a position visible from the main lane of traffic. Side caps facing the main traffic flow outsell opposite-facing side caps by a factor of five.

The key to an effective layout for your antique store is to design a system that takes advantage of shoppers' natural propensity to move right, avoid bending over, and look straight ahead. By arranging your store's fixtures in a fashion that directs traffic flow, keeps high-profit items in the most visible locations, and varies the inventory's shelf placement, you can keep customers in your store longer and increase sales.

Mastering Bidding Behavior Helps Buyers Buy Lower and Sellers Sell Higher

L et's face it, the fun in surfing eBay isn't just found in bidding. Winning is even more fun, provided that you don't pay too much. Therein lies the danger in auction bidding: You can always win if you must. All you have to do is outbid the competition. But, winning doesn't always mean paying a higher price. Outbidding the competition is as much about strategy as it is about price.

That being the case, what's your auction bidding strategy? At live auctions, are you a "stealth" bidder, who bids with a wink, a nod or a surreptitious wave? Or do you bid aggressively, hoping to scare off the competition? What's your online bidding style? Are you a sniper or a squatter? Do you bid online using the same style of bidding that you use at a live auction? When you offer your own online auctions, can you tell where your price will end up by the type of bidders you are attracting? Like most everything else in our taxpayer-funded search for the truth, academia has thoroughly researched these topics and we're going to have a look at some of their results.

A few years ago, Jeffrey Ely and Tanjim Hossain of Northwestern University conducted field tests on the popular bidding strategy of "sniping" to determine if it was an effective bidding tool. Their results were presented in the paper "Sniping and Squatting in Auction Markets."

Having been on both sides of the gavel at live auctions, and both a buyer and seller on eBay, I've seen or used most of the techniques they discuss. Some of the techniques are effective, but some don't apply to the antiques business. One thing is certain when it comes to auction bidding: Understanding bidding behavior can help buyers buy lower and sellers sell higher. So let's dig in and see how we can become better bidders.

First, some definitions are in order.

For those unfamiliar with auction sniping, it's the online auction equivalent of military sniping. It's the S.W.A.T. team of auction bidding. When the winning bid in your auction comes from "out of nowhere," you have been sniped. Bidders never know when a sniper electronically lurks in the background until, in the final few seconds of an auction, the sniper's bid is automatically entered by sniping software. Other bidders simply can't respond fast enough to get in a manual bid that tops the sniped bid. Providing that the sniped bid is the highest, it wins the auction suddenly and aggressively.

One thing is certain when it comes to auction bidding: Understanding bidding behavior can help buyers buy lower and sellers sell higher.

Sniping only works with online auctions that have a definite ending time (a "hard close"). In a live auction, the bidding goes on for as long as there are bids and until the auctioneer declares the item sold. Some online auction platforms (most notably Amazon) use a "soft close" and extend an auction's closing time until several minutes have passed without a bid. You can't snipe those auctions.

Auction squatters are the opposite of auction snipers: They enter an auction early and take up residence until the bidding ends. Squatters bid early and often. They respond to competing bids by posting bids manually.

Ely and Hossain make a strong case in favor of squatting, and claim that the strategy produces a "competition effect." On a platform like eBay, which can have dozens of concurrent auctions for goods that are essentially the same, squatting an auction sends a clear message to would-be bidders: Stay away. Why would a bidder choose to participate in an auction that has multiple bidders, when there is likely a similar auction with less competition elsewhere? Competition drives up prices, and the best price will be found at an auction with fewer bidders. Unfortunately, when the item offered for sale is rare or collectible there aren't any competing auctions to go to. When that's the case there's no way to avoid competition from squatters and sniping becomes a valuable bidding strategy.

The rise in price that results from multiple bidders in a squatted auction is called the "escalation effect." Sniping such auctions is beneficial to buyers because the typical online squatter bids as if they were at a live auction: i.e., they respond to competing bids by manually placing a higher bid. Bidding early against such a bidder results in an escalating price because the squatter will continually place higher bids. Sniping reduces visible competition and results in a lower price.

Auction squatters don't like sniping; they claim that it isn't fair. Snipers respond by saying that auction squatters are naive and don't understand online auctions. My experience is that whether the auction is live or online, squatted or sniped, the prize goes to the highest bidder. Ely and Hossain agree. In their trials, sniping afforded about a 1 percent advantage over squatting in bidding on consumer goods. I suspect that sniping would hold a bigger advantage if the auctions were for antiques and collectibles.

Although sniping and squatting were in a statistical dead heat for which is the most advantageous bidding strategy, I came away from my reading with a few usable bidding tips:

1. If there are multiple auctions being conducted for the item you are seeking, choose the one with no bidders and squat.

2. If you decide to squat, be aggressive about it. Don't bid the minimum amount; doing so just invites competition. Instead, bid a significant percentage of what you are ultimately willing to pay.

3. If there are no similar auctions but there are multiple bidders, then snipe the auction. Set up the snipe with your maximum bid and then leave it alone. You'll either win it or you won't.

4. If you decide to neither snipe nor squat, don't bid until 90 percent of the auctions time allowance has passed. Thirty percent of an auction's bids are placed in the last 5 percent of the auction's lifetime.

Clinging to Outdated Descriptions May Be Hurting Your Antiques Business

"When I use a word," Humpty Dumpty said in rather a scornful tone, "it means just what I choose it to mean — neither more nor less."

"The question is," said Alice, "whether you can make words mean so many different things."

"The question is," said Humpty Dumpty, "which is to be master — that's all."
– Lewis Carroll, *Through the Looking Glass*

In our information-heavy, digitally driven world of antiques, dealers have learned to choose their words wisely. No one wants to risk bad feedback from an online buyer or a lawsuit from a disgruntled auction bidder because they have mislabeled an item. We know the difference between "antique," "vintage," collectible," and "retro." Or do we? And if you have answered that with an enthusiastic "I certainly do know the difference!" then listen up: this is for you. You may not know as much as you think you do. In fact, clinging to outdated words and definitions may be hurting your business.

Consider this: "Antique" is now an offensive verb, as in "I totally antiqued that guy!" (This may be peripherally related to the tacky furniture painting technique called "antiquing," but I digress.) In the modern usage defined by Urban Dictionary, the verb "antique" means to toss flour, sugar or another type of powder in someone's face — usually while the target is sleeping — to make it appear that a great deal of time has passed. Some variations also call for covering the victim's body with the powder, which can cause a fair amount of discomfort. This nonstandard definition of antique — which coincidentally is the least offensive one listed — can be traced to "Jackass," a reality TV prank and stunt show that also spawned several movies. (I will avoid the other definitions related to "antique," as none of them should be printed in a family publication.)

Contrast "antique" with the word "vintage." All the Urban Dictionary definitions surrounding the word "vintage" were positive. It seems that, to the younger generations, vintage is "cool," and antiques are not. Antiques are great-grandma's smelly old junk.

Among the young, the word "antique" has fallen out of favor. The traditional meaning of antique was nowhere to be found in Urban Dictionary. What does this mean for your business? By association, antiques stores are not cool. Why would young professionals go into an antiques store if antiques are not desirable?

Say you have essentially the same inventory as the vintage store across the street. Which store is going to attract young professionals? The vintage store, because the customer is pre-disposed to shop there.

Words have power. Words are convincing. Words are the building blocks of thought. Consumers attach an emotional charge to words and use those emotions to guide their buying decisions. "Antique" is apparently a negatively charged word to many of your future customers.

Sally Schwartz of Chicago's Randolph Street Market Festival puts it like this: "It's a marketing issue, because the word 'antique' connotes — for people who don't know — old and smelly ... But when they hear the word 'retro' or 'vintage,' young people get excited, because that's what is very hip right now. Movie stars are carrying vintage handbags and dressing in designer clothes from the '60s and '70s ... The strategy is straightforward: to have a different look for a different audience."

There's an entire science dedicated to choosing marketing words to target certain consumers (there is always someone willing to finance marketing research). The science, called Semantic Differential, measures consumer's attitudes toward stimulus words, objects and concepts among different age groups, cultures and languages. The semantics of "antique" vs. "vintage" has moved away from the retail floor and into university laboratories.

The question then is "Who are you marketing to?" rather than "What are you selling?"

Most dealers carry a mix of antiques, collectibles and vintage goods. If all of your advertising emphasizes "antiques," you probably aren't attracting many new young customers. Perhaps the word "antique" is even part of your business name. What message does this send? What customers does the word attract? How old are they? Will these customers still be viable in 10, 15 or 20 years? How long do you want to stay in business, and who will your customers be 10 years from now?

Is it necessary for you to reposition your business as a "vintage" store? No, it's not. Antiques and collectibles are still in demand; they're just not in demand with younger buyers. The problem that presents to antiques businesses is that their customer base isn't growing as fast as it could. Younger customers are shopping vintage stores, not antiques stores. Here are a few ideas on how to capture vintage buyers without making a major change to your business:

1. If you sell at outside shows and fairs, choose venues that aren't exclusively promoted as "antiques" events, such as arts and crafts shows, major flea markets, boat shows and music or food festivals. These events will attract a different clientele. Make sure your merchandise complements the venue.

We know the difference between "antique," "vintage," collectible," and "retro." Or do we?

Show primarily vintage goods instead of a lot of antiques. You want to establish your store as the place to shop for vintage items while still leaving a door open to show and sell antiques. After all, everything has a vintage, even antiques. Track the profitability of these events by modifying your accounting to include a profit center for the outside venues where you promote vintage goods. In your customer database, create a field that identifies customers obtained from outside venues so you can track customer growth from such events.

2. Segment your print advertising. Limit your advertising for "antiques" to publications that are read by the 45-50+ demographic. When you advertise

in publications that have a younger readership, emphasize that you're a vintage seller, and advertise your vintage goods. Include a coupon or premium in such ads so you can track where your new customers are coming from.

3. Hold an in-store contest that encourages participants to come into your store to identify a group of antiques and vintage objects (make it difficult, but not impossible). Offer a substantial prize, like a $500 shopping spree at your store (your cost: around $200), event tickets or something else enticing. In your contest ads, show a picture of just one of the items; you'll be surprised how many people will say, "I know what that is!" and come down to your store to have a look at your other items.

Alice was correct: Words mean many different things. To paraphrase Humpty Dumpty's question, who will be the master (of the words that define our business)? We can be the masters — as long as we use the power of words to capture the attention and interest of new customers. If we don't, we'll end up like Humpty Dumpty, where all the king's horses and all the king's men can't put our businesses back together again.

Affordable Tips for Promoting Your Antiques Business

A mong antiques dealers, hope springs eternal. Dealers look forward to a new year, hoping for profitable merchandise, good inventory turnover, and new customers. Some dealers will spend the year hoping; others will make a plan and work to make the plan a reality.

Central to gaining more customers and making more sales is building store traffic. Antiques dealers have the same challenges as other retailers: how to build awareness for their business and get more customers in the door. I'll share some promotions that retailers in other businesses have successfully used; perhaps a few of them will work for you, too.

1. **Create space for community/club events**. This idea comes from a used bookseller in Maryland, who has a room behind his store that he loans to community groups for their meetings. Toastmasters, the local bridge club, and (of course) local book clubs all gather at his shop on a regular basis. He provides coffee and cookies for each meeting and makes it a point to get to know each of the club members, who invariably become regular customers and spread the word about new items.

2. **Get a radio show**. No, really; talk radio is popular, but this promotional concept doesn't involve creating a huge following by becoming a national radio star. Instead, the idea is to reach the friends and family of your existing customers. You know who your collectors are: interview them about their hobby. Just get them talking about how they got started, what they look

for, etc., and ask them a few relevant questions. Nothing fancy. Record the interview on a digital recorder, and upload the file to one of the dozens of Internet radio sites. Many of the sites will help you get set up, and the cost is miniscule compared to traditional radio. Your collector will tell everyone they know that they're "going to be interviewed on the radio," and all of their friends and relatives will tune in to listen. Get them to post a link on Facebook so you can increase your message's range. You and your store will become a hit with your collector's inner circle.

3. **Write a book**. This is easier than it sounds. When you interviewed your collectors for your radio show, you got them to release the rights to you. If you simply compile your interviews into a book form, you have a book. Use the book to build your mailing list: Offer it to customers in your store or as a free digital download

This year, decide to try something new to build your store traffic and then follow through with your decision.

on your website or blog. Being a published author lends credibility to your expertise, and will likely get you an interview with the local radio station or newspaper. If you're unsure of your writing skills, you can find ghostwriters and editors online.

4. **Start an article marketing campaign**. Turn your expertise into Google page rank for your website by writing articles and posting them to online article directories. Articles that are written well, timely, and keyword-oriented can show up on the first page of Google within hours. Why? Because people are looking for the information. Article writing works well for those who give thoughtful consideration to their articles, assemble them correctly, and distribute them effectively. Best of all, the articles stay around for years and continually publicize your business.

5. **Sponsor a sports prize**. Chances are good that your town has amateur sports teams. For the cost of a small insurance premium, you can offer a cash prize for a hole-in-one, a grand slam home run, or bowling a 300 game. Car dealerships use this promotion regularly. The concept of prize indemnifica-

tion includes almost every type of event that involves an element of chance and skill. Pick a well-attended local event and you will likely be interviewed on radio, TV, and newspapers. For the price, you can't buy that kind of press coverage.

6. **Take your show on the road**. Pity the poor civic club program planners: They have to find new speakers and presenters for every meeting. Rotary, Lions, Garden Club, and others are constantly on the lookout for new speakers. Assemble a 10-minute PowerPoint presentation that explains the history, usage, and points of connoisseurship for one of your favorite items, and I guarantee clubs will invite you to speak.

7. **Take advantage of bad weather**. Whenever snow starts to fall, radio stations crank up their bad weather openings/closings reports. Is your store closed? Is your store open? Either way, chances are good that your local radio station will announce your decision, and plug your business at the same time.

8. **Charge for your seminars**. Be honest: What sort of turnout do you get at your free seminars? The general public believes that free seminars are worth every penny you charge for them: zip. Here's an interesting twist: Events like these are better attended if you charge for them. Also, stop calling them seminars. The word is overused. Instead, call them clinics. Bring in a paid expert and charge admission. You'll get more people and might make a few bucks in the process.

9. **Let the public know that you are traffic friendly**. Did you ever notice that stores post signs for what they won't do? NO bathrooms, NO meter change, etc. Instead, post signs if you are willing to give change or give the public access to your restrooms. If you don't want to offer your facilities, please don't post any signs at all; nothing deters traffic more than an unfriendly sign posted in your window.

10. **Join the parade**. Parades attract big crowds and typically have no entry fees. Most dealers have access to a utility trailer, which can be turned into a rolling advertisement. Your float decorations can be reused year after year. Parades are one of the cheapest goodwill-builders that a dealer can employ.

11. **Cross-promote**. Team up with a non-competing but complementary store and display each other's products. Some prefer to call this arrangement a strategic alliance. Whatever it's called, the idea has been around for years. It's still being used because it is still effective. Each retailer is exposed to the customer base of the partner store. The key to success here is to choose your partner carefully. The cross-promotion has to make sense in the mind of the customer. No retailer ever has enough creative display ideas. Many stores borrow antique furniture to lend a certain look to their store. Look at all the stores around your community to see which would be a good fit for a cross-promotion.

Dealers, this year decide to try something new to build your store traffic and then follow through with your decision. These suggestions are all low-cost ideas and may produce new customers. One thing's for sure: If you want to see different results in 2011, you will have to try something new.

Occupy Main Street: How Antiques Dealers Can Boost the Shop Local Movement

No matter what you think of the Occupy Wall Street movement, it holds the seed of successful sales for antique dealers.

The Wall Street protestors have expressed frustration with taxpayer bailouts of "too big to fail" corporations who take public tax money and then raise banking fees, restrict access to loans, and then give their CEOs big bonuses. Versions of Occupy Wall Street spread across the United States, and then to 951 European cities and 82 countries around the world. The public is endorsing the message: Institutions and individuals are moving their money to hometown banks. Hometown banks have seen out-of-the-ordinary surges in deposits in the past several months.

Not only are individual citizens fed up with the too big to fail mentality of the banking conglomerates, state governments are as well. Lawmakers in Maryland, Massachusetts, New Mexico, and Minnesota have all voted to move state funds into local banks and credit unions. Labor unions, small businesses, and municipalities are also moving funds to local institutions.

The anti-big-bank, anti-big-corporation mindset is throwing fuel on the fire of the buy local movement. Bloggers are writing about buying local, as are major newspapers and media outlets. Michael Shuman, author of *The Small-Mart Revolution* says: "In the current economic downturn, Americans are beginning to understand that their future prosperity lies in the community businesses down the street that employ their neighbors, pay the taxes, and promote local relationships and trust."

Economic-localism is a growing grassroots movement. Since the recession began four years ago, the Business Alliance for Local Living Economies has grown to more than 60 small business networks in the United States, representing more than 20,000 entrepreneurs.

What does this mean for antiques dealers? Consumers are getting the buy local message. They are more inclined now to buy local than they were three or four years ago.

They will still shop at big-box stores, but if you give them sufficient reason to shop at your store they will do so, and get the added benefit of feeling like they have contributed to the local economy.

Remember, you offer one-of-a-kind, unique gifts that can't be purchased at a big-box store. Capitalize on that. Now is a good time to get new customers and boost your mailing list. A new customer over the holidays may become a regular customer for the rest of the year.

Getting new holiday customers requires a two-pronged strategy:

Consumers will still shop at big-box stores, but if you give them sufficient reason to shop at your store, they will.

1. Get them to your store.

2. Help them enjoy the experience once they're there.

You're already familiar with the standard ways of promoting your business over the holidays, so I won't review them again. Instead, let's investigate a new tactic for getting customers into your store and starting the season off with a bang.

In 2010, American Express started a Small Business Saturday promotion, in which consumers were offered incentives for shopping at local small businesses on the day after Black Friday (the day after Thanksgiving). According to American Express, participating small businesses saw a 28 percent rise in sales on that Saturday compared to the same day in 2009.

In 2011, Amex joined Facebook, Google, Twitter, and others to offer a small business toolkit that enables merchants to tie into the national Small Business Saturday campaign. The toolkit included:

$100 in free Facebook ads for the first 10,000 business owners who sign up. Facebook ads will enable you to laser-target collectors in your local community.

The video creation tool My Business Story, which enables business owners to create professional-quality videos for posting to YouTube and other social networks.

$100 credit for LinkedIn.com ads and an additional $100 in Facebook ad credits for up to 6,500 businesses from YourBuzz, a business review site.

Downloadable, customizable point-of-purchase displays to let consumers know that a merchant is participating in the promotion.

Customizable email templates for Christmas email campaigns.

When holiday shoppers arrive, give them an experience that they can't get in a big-box store. Offer a festive, down-home, comfortable atmosphere that is conducive to lingering and browsing. Make it a sensory experience: use sight, sound, smell, and/or taste.

When a customer walks into your store, let them smell potpourri or cinnamon and cloves (avoid the smell of pine, it smells like household cleaner). "Christmassy" smells will trigger memories of home and family and put shoppers in a nostalgic mood. Every real estate agent knows that the smell of cookies baking increases the chance of a showing turning into a sale. Why not use the same tactic in your store?

Offer tasty snacks: cookies, mulled cider, candy or breads will be appreciated by hungry shoppers. Remember, a hungry shopper doesn't shop very long. The treats don't have to be offered every hour you are open; perhaps just on your primary selling days or during a holiday open house.

Try live music. A guitar player or vocal duet singing holiday carols will be a welcome change to big box canned music.

Make a colorful visual display of "Christmas past." This sort of display is ideally suited for antiques and collectibles dealers, and will add to the nostalgic mood.

Here are a few other ideas that dealers have employed to increase their holiday sales:

Offer value added packages to increase the average dollar sale. Display items that go together and offer a package price on the group.

Advertise your hours well. If your store is in a business district that shuts down at 6 p.m., consider opening early instead of staying late. Customers will enjoy a before-work shopping experience (be sure to provide coffee and pastries).

With special items, give away a nicely typed and formatted story about the item. Such a certificate can turn any item into a conversation piece and be remembered for years.

Regardless of the state of the economy, shoppers will spend money. But they will be more careful about what they spend. Of primary concern to shoppers is the impact of the gifts that they buy, rather than price or quantity.

Why Antiques Shop Rents Should Be Based on Location, Traffic

Why do shows and shops tell dealers they are selling space when they are really selling traffic?

Who pays for traffic?

A well-worn aphorism is that there are but three important considerations in real estate: location, location, and location. I submit that this isn't true for antiques dealers. For antiques dealers, the three most important considerations are location, traffic, and lease. Within each of these three categories are variables that can mean the difference between a dealer's outstanding success and dismal failure.

Location, for example, doesn't just refer to the location of the building you're in. A small dealer (Vendor A) who has a booth inside a well-located antique mall but whose booth is located in a poorly trafficked aisle benefits less from the mall's location than the other dealers in the mall. If Vendor A pays the same booth rent as a vendor in a better-trafficked part of the mall (Vendor B), then Vendor A has a bad lease. Compared to Vendor B, Vendor A is overpaying for rent because he has too little traffic. If Vendor A pays rent consisting of a base rent plus a percentage of sales, his situation worsens. Which dealer is likely to still be in business in two years: Vendor A or Vendor B?

I'm going to stick my neck out and boldly state that antique malls (and antique shows) that rent space based solely on booth size are cheating themselves and their dealers.

Dealers, what are you paying for when you rent booth space at a mall or a show? Storage space for your merchandise? Of course not. If you want to store your inventory, use a storage locker. You're paying for traffic; you're paying for customers to see and purchase your goods.

Mall managers, what are you selling to your vendors? Space? If that's what you think you're selling then you need to take a closer look at your business model. You, too, are selling traffic. Your facility and your advertising budget should be configured to maximize traffic. The dealers who benefit most from your traffic should pay the most rent. And, you should cut a rent break to dealers who are stuck in no

For antiques dealers, the three most important considerations are location, traffic and lease.

man's land. Also, if a dealer has his own advertising budget or sells merchandise that is a draw for your mall, he should pay less rent than a dealer who depends on the mall to deliver traffic to his booth.

The above suggestions are based on the model used by management companies at regional commercial malls. Professional management companies who run malls – those with anchor stores like Sears and JC Penney – recognize that all sections of their malls are not equally trafficked and they price them accordingly. Commercial malls charge for traffic first, space second. Space adjacent to an anchor store or in the main traffic lane is priced higher than space in the corridor leading to the restrooms or an exit. Anchor stores that supply traffic to the mall pay lower rent than the specialty retailers who benefit from the traffic the anchors generate. The key is traffic: where it comes from, and who delivers it. Gould, Pashigan and Prendergast in their study, "Contracts, Externalities, and Incentives in Shopping Malls" explain that even though the big anchor stores take up most of the space in a mall (on average, 58 percent) they pay less rent (an average of 10 percent, though some anchors pay no rent at all). Anchor stores get a huge "rent break" because they are a draw for the mall and have huge advertising budgets.

How can antique malls maximize their rents while simultaneously leveling the playing field for their vendors? By using a traffic counter. There are many available (Google search phrase: "mall traffic counter") and it's a small investment considering the return. A wireless traffic counter will not only tell you how many customers you get into your mall, but where they go once they're in. When you know where your traffic is going (and where it's not going) you can re-arrange your booth layout to draw traffic to where you want it to go.

Why do grocery stores put meat and dairy in the back of the store? Because most folks buy meat and dairy, and will work their way through aisles of other merchandise to get to the meat department. How many shoppers would go to the back of the store if meat, bread and dairy were displayed up front? Not as many. Having an accurate customer count provides other benefits as well; with it you can track the effectiveness of your advertising and plan your staffing needs based on a metric other than sales.

Here's how to figure your rents based on traffic: Divide your space into zones and keep a traffic count in each zone for each selling season. The zones with the highest average annual traffic count should have the highest base rent. Zones with the lowest traffic count will have the lowest base rents. If you offer your dealers a percentage lease, then the amount you collect will raise as sales rise, and sales will definitely rise.

Mall managers, you've spent a lot of money to get customers into your mall. Don't you want them to spend some time there and see as much merchandise as possible? A half of a percent in sales improvement can mean thousands of dollars for you and your vendors. Such an increase – and more – can be achieved with your existing customer base. All you have to do is re-arrange your booths and adjust your rents.

How do you keep vendors from kicking and screaming about their booths being moved or their rents being raised? (None will argue about their rent being lowered.) You don't. You will almost certainly lose a few vendors. If you take a year to track traffic flow (and you should if you want an accurate count), keep the dealers in the loop regarding the upcoming change so they will have time to get used to the idea.

Once the change is in place, vendors will see that they are more profitable because their rent will be a smaller percentage of sales, and that will make everyone happy.

If you price your booth rent according to traffic flow rather than square footage, you'll find that your dealers will be more profitable, and with profitable vendors, you'll have less turnover and fewer associated headaches.

How Better Tags Help You Exceed Customers' Expectations

Sitting in his cell awaiting trial for treason, Van Meegeren considered his options. The year was 1945, and the war was over. Meegeren had been arrested in his Dutch homeland for being a Nazi collaborator. His crime, according to Dutch authorities, was trading a painting by Dutch artist Johannes Vermeer to the Nazi commander of the Luftwaffe, Hermann Goering. Collaborating with the enemy was a capital offense. If convicted, Meegeren would hang.

At his trial, Meegeren offered a novel defense: that he had, in fact, painted the Vermeer himself. It was a forgery. In return for his forgery, he acquired from Goering six genuine paintings by Dutch masters. Meegeren had conned Goering. Meegeren asserted that he was, therefore, a national hero and not a Nazi collaborator.

To prove his defense, Meegeren painted another Vermeer before the court while under police guard. Compared to Vermeer, Meegeren's technique was clumsy; but with the aid of a new product called Bakelite, Meegeren produced a satisfactory forgery. He was convicted of forgery and exonerated of the treason charge. He was sentenced to a year in jail.

Why was Van Meegeren able to avoid the hangman's noose? Because his painting met the critic's expectations of what a Vermeer should look like.

According to Yale psychology professor Paul Bloom, "expectation" shapes our entire sensory experience and is directly responsible for creating our sense of pleasure. In his book *How Pleasure Works: The New Science of Why We Like What We Like*, Bloom states that it "is not the world [that impacts] our senses. Rather, the enjoyment we get from something derives from what we think that thing is."

Bloom offers much research to support his assertion:

Gourmets were invited to sample canned dog food, which was presented to them as pate de fois gras. They loved it.

Researchers swapped the labels of several expensive French wines with ordinary California table wines. At the tasting, wine experts extolled the expensively labeled California wine while few liked the cheaply labeled but better quality French wine.

Bloom goes on to cite examples relating to sports, sex, cannibalism, art, music, religion, and yes, antiques and collectibles. At the heart of his argument is humanity's apparently deeply rooted but subconscious tendency to believe that objects are imbued with a sort of "invisible essence," by their owners and/or creators.

A Vermeer is imbued with the essence of Vermeer. A tape measure that belonged to John F. Kennedy is imbued with the essence of JFK. Even if the Vermeer is a forgery and the tape measure belonged to Wayne Jordan, if your expectation is that you are admiring the real thing, your enjoyment of the experience is measurably enhanced.

If Bloom is correct, antiques dealers are not selling objects, they are selling stories. The inventory item is simply the physical representation of the story.

Antiques dealers have long known that documented provenance or a good story adds value to an item; such knowledge can be put to better use in most antique stores, though. Consider this scenario: a customer walks into your store. A

Antique dealers are not selling objects, they are selling stories. The inventory item is simply the physical representation of the story.

staff member greets them, and asks the usual question: "Can I help you?" or some variation thereof. What's the customer's response? "Just looking."

What will they be looking at? Your merchandise, signage, and price tags. If, as Bloom suggests, objects can be imbued with an "invisible essence" that makes them more appreciated, why not create signage and price tags that enhance your customer's experience and enjoyment of the items in your inventory? Here are a few ideas on how to build a customer's level of appreciation for the items in your store:

Use shelf cards to describe the item; tell what makes the item special and collectible. Wine merchants have been using this tactic for years. A recent study by the Ehrenberg-Bass Institute for Marketing Science (EBI) suggests that consumers lack sufficient expertise in wine to make a purchase decision based solely on a wine's style, region, and vintage. Instead, they rely on information provided on the label and on the shelf to guide their choice. Likewise, most buyers of collectibles are not "sophisticated" buyers.

Put the item's price on the shelf card. Don't let a price stand alone; most customers won't relate the price to the value. Tell them where the value lies.

Make an educational display for your primary profit centers. Museums do this. Tell your customers the points of connoisseurship for your various types of glassware, for example. Then make sure that your shelf cards reflect the information provided in your displays.

Arm your sales staff with stories about the provenance of your inventory items.

If you pre-educate your shoppers, here's what you can expect to happen:

- Shopping in your store (or even just browsing) will be perceived as being more fun than shopping in your competitor's store.

- Customers will perceive more value in your inventory items.

- You can increase your retail price on many items.

- Higher starting prices will give you more room to move when it comes down to negotiating the final selling price.

- Your overall profit margins will increase.

- Your inventory will turn faster, increasing your return on investment.

- You can get more "marketing mileage" by featuring your inventory items in press releases and YouTube videos.

Big corporations spend a lot of money to learn what makes consumers buy. Universities worldwide offer degrees in the art and science of merchandising. Much research has been done proving that consumers in a retail store behave in predictable ways.

If a dealer knows ahead of time that his customers will enter his store, stop near the door, move to the right and be affected by shiny displays and shelf cards, wouldn't it make sense to capitalize on this behavior?

If there's one thing you can count on, it's that antiques stores will attract lookers. Antiques stores are surrogate museums. People sometimes browse in them for entertainment. Why not take advantage of the "just looking" response to pre-sell your customers?

Like Van Meergeren, create an expectation in your customers. Let them learn to expect quality merchandise and a certain level of enlightenment and education when they enter your store. If you do, you will see them more often and sell them more merchandise.

Antiques Shop Surveillance Tools Should Be on Everyone's Radar

It was just after 7 a.m., and the Mountain Top Antique Mall in Hillsville, Va., hadn't opened yet. A late-model black pickup truck pulled into the mall's lot and parked. An older man got out of the truck, walked up to the porch and tried the door; it was locked. No one was around and the location wasn't easily visible from the road. The man helped himself to about $150 worth of the hanging flower baskets that decorated the mall's front porch, loaded them into his truck and drove away. There were no witnesses.

Two days later, the police arrested the man responsible for the robbery. How?

The entire incident was recorded June 17, 2012 on video by one of Mountain Top's three security systems. After reporting the incident to the police, Travis Griffin, the store manager, and Jonathan Dillman, the store's information technology specialist, assembled a video of the robbery and posted it to YouTube and the store's Facebook page (security camera footage and narration can be seen at http://tinyurl.com/MountainTopTheft). The video was picked up by the local newspaper, *The Galax Gazette*, which reported the robbery and asked for help identifying the thief. Readers responded, and a suspect was arrested.

Such thefts are commonplace. The National Association for Shoplifting Prevention (NASP) reports that more than 10 million people have been caught shoplifting in the last five years. Imagine how many are not getting caught! Shoplifters report that they are caught only once in every 48 times they steal. Police are only involved 50 percent of the time, so even the statistics that are kept are not the full picture. Add in the cost of employee theft — 58 percent of all retail theft — and inventory shrinkage becomes a very big expense for retailers.

Who's stealing? Every age group and social demographic of men, women and children. There is no "typical shoplifter" profile. Nationwide, one in every 11 people has shoplifted; that's approximately 27 million shoplifters. Shoplifters usually buy and steal merchandise in the same visit, and they typically steal $2 to $200 worth of merchandise per incident. NASP studies indicate that shoplifting is a compulsion; it's addicting in the same way drugs are. The thrill of "getting away with it" releases endorphins in the brain that produce what shoplifters describe as a "rush" or "high." NASP reports that it's this high — not the merchandise itself — that compels shoplifters to steal; 57 percent of adults and 33 percent of juveniles say it is hard for them to stop shoplifting even after getting caught.

The antiques shops I interviewed for this article fell mostly into two categories: antiques malls, like Mountain Top, which go to great lengths to protect their consignors' merchandise, and mom-and-pop stores that have no security systems at all. Understandably, the operations without security systems didn't want to be identified; to do so would be like posting a neon sign that reads "Shoplifters Welcome." Some small, single-owner shops have security systems, but not many. Often, antiques shops occupy re-zoned residential space rather than commercial retail space. The many small rooms of a former residence require more cameras and security precautions than an open commercial space, so setting up a state-of-the-art security system can be expensive. Smaller shop owners say that their low level of theft doesn't justify the cost of an expensive security system.

Security systems don't have to be expensive to be effective. Cameras don't even have to work at all to deter theft. But if your cameras don't work, you won't catch any thieves. Just ask the folks at Mountain Top Antique Mall.

"The problem with cameras," says Jeff Budd of Smartwire Security & Surveillance in Jacksonville, Fla., "is that someone has to be watching them (in order to catch a shoplifter). Otherwise, you may have to go through hours of video to find the theft."

By that time, the thief is long gone. Budd, whose wife was an antiques dealer for 40 years, is very familiar with the security needs of antique stores.

Cameras are a good general deterrent, but stores' biggest losses come from unsecured showcases, according to Budd.

The bigger the mall, the bigger the problem. Dealers usually put their most expensive items (jewelry, coins, etc.) into a locked showcase, thinking that the goods are safe. Certainly they are safe from casual shoplifters, but determined thieves know that showcases hold the pricier items, and they have ways to quickly "jimmy" the door lock or use a suction cup to break through the glass. Budd recommends that showcases be equipped with a security device that sounds at the register any time a showcase door opens.

Surveillance cameras should be part of an overall security system, but dealers shouldn't rely on them entirely. Today, there are security systems available that guard against almost any contingency, but many of them would be of no use to an antiques dealer (like individual electronically monitored clothing tags, for example). Some security systems are closed systems, and some connect to the Internet for remote surveillance.

Smaller shop owners say that their low level of theft doesn't justify the cost of an expensive security system. But security systems don't have to be expensive to be effective.

Here are some of the most common security measures shops are using today:

DVR and cameras

DVR (digital video recorder) systems include the DVR and a choice of dome, bullet, C-mount or infrared cameras; the DVR power supply; and one or more monitors. Most cameras come in both indoor and outdoor models. The camera viewing area should cover all points of entry and sensitive store areas. Security system consultants can help to identify where the cameras should be placed in your store. Sets can cost north of $200 for a four-camera outfit.

Fake cameras

Fake cameras have been referred to as "scarecrow surveillance." Like a scarecrow in a garden, they are designed to discourage theft. Thieves don't like to be seen, and if they think they are being watched, they will steal somewhere else. The best fake cameras look like the real thing: they have flashing LED lights, motion sensors and move in the direction of motion. Most operate on batteries; if yours does, be sure to change the batteries regularly. One camera can cost as little as $15.

Signage

Signage falls into the category of scarecrow surveillance. Strategically placed signs that read "Smile, You're on Camera," "Shoplifters Will Be Prosecuted" and security company logos on doors and windows are common. Signs cost about $10 each.

Fisheye mirrors

Convex "fisheye" mirrors are a cost-effective way to make blind spots visible. But, as Jeff Budd pointed out, someone has to be watching them. These mirrors cost $20 to $100, depending on size.

Door chimes

Almost everyone uses these to alert the staff that someone has entered or left the store. Found nearly everywhere, these chimes cost about $30 for a single set.

1 sound enter
2nd sound for exit

Showcase alarms

Common mainly in antiques malls that have many vendors and showcases, these alarms cost from $12 to as much as $100, depending on style and function.

Intrusion detection

The first line of defense for a retail store is door and window security. Most of the dealers I spoke with had some sort of monitored burglar alarm system. A whole-shop system for doors and windows can run as much as $300.

When I asked Mountain Top Antique Mall's Travis Griffin what that business' most effective shoplifting deterrent was, he replied, "The publicity we have received from this incident. Once the public knows we are serious about security, shoplifters will stay away."

Of course, dealers should not wait for a robbery before they get the word out about their security. A well-displayed combination of functional, "scarecrow" and old-fashioned fisheye mirrors and door chimes will send a clear message to potential shoplifters that they should get their thrills someplace else.

Don't Let Sales Get Thrown Under the Bus for Lack of Savvy Customer Interaction

American popular culture loves a catchphrase. Always has. In the 1890s, businessmen were anxious to "get down to brass tacks," and a well-heeled customer who was satisfied with his purchases was "as happy as a clam." In the 1990s, if a customer discovered that a dealer's claims were all smoke and mirrors, then the deal "went down the tubes," and it was "hasta la vista, baby."

Dealers thrown under the bus

The latest popular catchphrase — "thrown under the bus" — was originally used by sports writers. Referring to the team bus, an athlete was either in favor (on the bus) or out of favor (under the bus). The recent economic environment has made the phrase a favorite of politicians and financial writers. *Washington Post* writer David Segal called the expression "the cliché of the 2008 (Presidential) campaign."

"Thrown under the bus" has come to mean the sacrifice of a person who doesn't deserve to be sacrificed. For example, consider the way customers sometimes treat antiques dealers (or other retailers):

Customer enters store.

Dealer: "Can I help you?"

Customer: "Just looking."

Dealer walks away.

Thrown under the bus. Sacrificed undeservedly, the dealer resumes his or her position behind the counter and wonders what to do next while the customer walks around the store, sneering at the price tags.

Two things to do after they say 'Just looking'

The call and response of "Can I help you/Just looking" is so ingrained in the retail experience that even when shoppers want help, they often respond with "Just looking." This is especially true in stores that sell discretionary items, like antiques stores. In stores that supply needed goods and services, the response to "Can I help you?" is often "Yes." "Yes, I need a haircut." "Yes, I need a new pair of jeans." "Yes, I need a new washing machine."

Let's get back to the drawing board and find a way to deal with the inevitable "just looking" response that doesn't involve "Can I help you?" or any of its derivatives.

When customers enters your store, it's important that you acknowledge them. Nothing annoys me more than to walk into a store, realize that I have been seen and no one has acknowledged my presence. I'm not suggesting that you employ the "Welcome to Wal-Mart" strategy. What works is to hit customers with a double whammy. Greet them, and then employ a pre-emptive strike, something like this:

> **Let's find a way to deal with the inevitable "just looking" response that doesn't involve "Can I help you?" or any of its derivatives.**

Customer enters store.

Dealer: "Hi, there. Have a look around, and I'll be right with you."

Bada-bing, bada-boom. Now they can't tell you that they're "just looking," because you have just given them your permission to look around. You've insisted on it, actually. Plus, you've established the fact that you intend to approach them in the near future to check their progress.

When the time comes to approach them, don't make a tactical blunder. Don't fall back into "So what can I help you with?" or "What can I do for you today?" Now isn't the time to be barking up the wrong tree. Be proactive. Keep the ball rolling. You're building a business. Your first objective is to make a sale, but if you don't make a sale, then your second objective is to build a relationship and gain a customer. Here are a couple of tactics for your consideration.

Ask an open-ended question

Let your customer "land." Give them time to browse for a few minutes, and then approach them when they've stopped to look at something. Using your best smile, ask an open-ended question. An open-ended question is one that cannot be answered with "yes" or "no." Examples: "What is it about this that caught your eye?" or "What sort of things do you collect?"

Open-ended questions reveal customers' motivations and interests. Their answers give you the information you need to find items that please them, negotiate a price and make a sale (or not). If you ask, "What brings you in today?" then you just might find that customers are killing time while their cars are serviced. At least you'll know where you stand.

The most valuable technique you can learn to improve your personal selling skills is to always ask open-ended questions. This is harder than it sounds. I once participated in a training exercise wherein salespeople paired off and interviewed one another. Participants were eliminated whenever they asked any question that could be answered "yes" or "no". It took less than five minutes to eliminate the entire class — more than 50 experienced salespeople.

Ask for their opinion

If you have a customer who is lingering but not landing, ask his opinion. Point out two nearby items and say, "I'd like to rearrange this counter. Which of these two items should be the focal point of this display?" or some other similarly innocuous question. No matter what they answer, reply with "Why?" In fact, if you find yourself getting a "no" response to any question, the best way to re-start the conversation is by asking "why?"

Your purpose is to engage the customer in conversation and break down the "You're not going to sell me anything" defenses. Consumers buy from people that they know, like and trust. If you engage them in conversation rather than pounce on them, they will be more comfortable being in your store.

Using the above suggestions, come up with your own questions and remarks that don't require "yes" or "no" responses. You don't need many — three or four approaches will do. The point is to break the "Can I help you"/"Just looking" habit.

Don't let your customers throw you under the bus. When you find something that works, write it down. Use it over and over. Teach it to your employees. Make it a habit, and make your employees make it a habit. Doing so will be a real shot in the arm for your business.

And that's the whole nine yards. Hasta la vista, baby.

What Antiques Dealers Can Learn From Junk Mail – Part 1

I have a confession: I am a junk mail junkie. Unlike most sensible people (you, perhaps?) who throw junk mail into the trash, I read everything. Offers for credit cards and insurance, car dealership flyers, coupon mailers, newspaper ads, and long-form sales letters get read from beginning to end. I've been doing it for 40 years. My mother would be so ashamed.

It's not that I have nothing to do and lots of time on my hands. My problem is that I am addicted to advertising. When I started my first business, I couldn't afford to hire an agency to develop my ads. So, I let the newspaper write my display ads for me. Big mistake. Perhaps *The Washington Post* has a good ad department, but my hometown newspaper did not. The ads that my local paper created were awful, and I decided that I could do better myself.

That's when I started analyzing other company's advertising. After all, banks and car manufacturers spend hundreds of thousands of dollars to develop and test each advertising piece. I could learn from their example. I studied headlines, sub-headings, paragraph headings, body content, offers and calls-to-action. Who was the ad aimed at? How did it get my attention? Did it hold my interest until the end? When I found something that I thought might work for my business, I placed the ad into my files for future reference. I also read all the copywriting books that I could get my hands on.

Antiques dealers and other small business owners can seldom afford to hire an agency to develop their ads. Like I did, they either write the ads themselves or have a friend, relative, employee, student, or ad sales rep write the ads for them. For this reason, small businesses ads are almost always poorly written and ineffective.

Nevertheless, small businesses are still in need of effective advertising. By following a few simple guidelines, antiques dealers can produce effective advertising copy that will have a positive effect on their sales.

My seventh-grade art teacher once told me, "Before you can accurately draw something, you must know what it looks like." Sound advice. Let's explore how a good ad reads. I'm not a graphic artist and am not qualified to discuss layout so I'll leave that subject on the table. My focus here will be how to deliver your message so that your ad will be noticed and read.

By following a few simple guidelines, antiques dealers can produce effective advertising copy that will have a positive effect on their sales.

Let's start with an example of a poorly written ad, and then see what we can do to improve upon it. A typical ad for an antiques dealer will use the business name as the headline and the business tag line or motto for the sub-heading. The body copy will consist of a list of services or inventory types. The ad will close with contact information, store address, and hours. Slightly better ads will contain an offer of some sort. I'm sure you've seen hundreds of ads that fit this description. Here's a fictional example:

Joe's Antiques

Always Accepting Quality Consignments

See Us For: Advertising, Sports Memorabilia, Toys

123 Main St. Anytown

Phone number

Hours

The above ad will, over time, build an awareness of Joe's business. What it won't do is bring customers into his store right now. Joe's ad makes the classic advertising mistake: He says what he wants to say, not what his customers want to hear. You see, no one gives a fig about Joe's business. The phone book is full of antiques dealers who provide exactly what Joe is advertising. How can Joe attract a reader's attention, develop interest in his store, build trust, and motivate his readers to act? Moreover, how can he do so in the space of a few sentences? To develop an effective ad, Joe must first answer a few questions:

Who is his audience?

What's the best way to reach them? If Joe wants to attract his existing customers, then an email or direct mail campaign will be cheaper and more effective than a newspaper display ad. If he wants to attract new customers, a newspaper ad is better, but he can't "shotgun" his ad. He needs to focus: What demographic is he attracting? What motivates the individuals in the demographic? The psychological truism "motivation affects perception" should be applied here. If Joe wants his ad to attract attention, he has to speak to the motivations of his target group.

What product will Joe offer?

What are the benefits of the product to Joe's target group? The second most common mistake dealers make in their ads is to list the features of their store or product rather than the benefits. Customers don't buy features, they buy benefits. There's an old sales training saw that goes, "No one buys an eighth-inch drill bit because they want a drill bit; they buy it because they want an eighth-inch hole." "Antique Toys" is a feature. "Relive the fun of your childhood" is a benefit related to antique toys.

What are his target customer's emotional triggers?

Customers buy on emotion, not logic. How do they feel when they collect a particular item? What emotional need is filled when someone buys Joe's featured product?

Does Joe have a testimonial that indicates that he has previously filled a customer's emotional need for his product? A July 2009 report from eConsultancy states that 90 percent of online consumers trust recommendations from people they know and 70 percent of consumers trust the opinions of unknown users. Testimonials build credibility; use them.

What offer can Joe make to motivate a customer to come into his store or visit his website?

An ad that does not contain an offer is a waste of money. Effective offers will be time-sensitive and offer some value to the targeted group. Offers don't always have to be based on lower prices; anything of value can be offered. The offer doesn't have to be one of Joe's products, either; it can be tickets to a ball game or entry into a drawing. One effective offer is to cross-promote with another related business, like a furniture store or such. The point is for Joe to give his customers a reason to come into his store now.

In the next section, we'll apply the above guidelines to our sample ad, and see what we come up with.

In the meantime, take a few minutes out of your day and have a look at the junk mail and ads that come your way. You never know when you'll find something that you can use.

What Antiques Dealers Can Learn From Junk Mail – Part 2

S o we've discussed the criteria for developing a good display ad. Let's apply the guidelines to our sample ad and see what we can come up with.

The most important part of a display ad is the headline. Headlines, whether online or in print, are written to grab the attention of "scanners." Consumers read headlines first, then sub-headings. If the headline piques the readers' interest, they will read your sub-heading. So your headline must be strong enough to attract attention away from all the competing ads on the page.

The sub-heading is the second most important part of your ad. In fishing terms, the sub-heading is where you "set the hook" – if you don't, the rest of your ad won't be read. So, let's first focus on how to write a good headline and sub-heading.

What will grab your reader's attention? Well, that depends on what the readers' motivations are. A headline that grabs the attention of a teenage boy probably won't appeal to a middle-aged woman. So the first thing to do when writing a headline is to decide whom you want your ad to appeal to. Who are your ideal customers? Who do you want to attract? What satisfaction will they get from your store and/or products?

The headline should appeal to your target group. Since you've already considered what satisfaction the target group will get from your store and/or featured product, build your headline around that concept. By doing so, you will have a headline that will most likely get their attention. One of the best ways to capture attention is by using a testimonial as a headline.

Creating a Headline Using a Testimonial

If you're already in the habit of collecting testimonials, chances are good that you have one that is headline material. Flip through your testimonials and look for a snippet of wording such as "Loved Your Selection!" or "We told our friends about you" or "I can't put it down!" Keep your target group and their "hot buttons" in mind. What you are looking for is an offbeat comment that you can distill into a few strong words. Those words can then be enlarged and used as an attention-getting headline. Not all testimonials are worthy of becoming headlines, but all are worthy of consideration.

If you don't already have a collection of testimonials, here's how to start one:

Build an infrastructure: Testimonials are more likely to be given if you provide opportunities for your customers to comment. Place a feedback form on your website, and a guestbook on your check-out counter.

> **Your headline must be strong enough to attract attention away from all the competing ads on the page.**

Ask for them: If you have taken the time to build long-term relationships with your customers, they are usually willing to give you a testimonial. This can be done in person or via email.

Keep your ears open: In all likelihood, you're already getting feedback on your products or services and are just not aware of it. Develop awareness for positive feedback, and write it down as it occurs. Say to the customer, "Can I quote you on that?"

Other headline options: You can also create a headline "hook" by asking a question, making a bold statement, or offering news (if you have made a special or rare acquisition). No matter how you craft your headline, make sure that it contains a benefit to your target group, either stated or implied. Your headline should answer the reader's question, "What's in it for me?"

The sub-heading: In the sub-heading you will expand on your headline to include the desires of your target group.

Writing the body copy

Don't go overboard here; you don't need to write a book. Make the ad easy to skim. Just hit the high points. The object is not to get the reader to click a "buy now" button, the object is to get them into your offline or online store. Give them enough information to accomplish that end and no more. Make it easy for readers to skim the ad and still get the message. Use bullets, sub-headings, bold text, or an eye-catching graphic.

How to Choose a Graphic

Remember the saying, "A picture is worth a thousand words?" That's still true today, even when you factor in inflation. Don't leave the graphic up to the newspaper's layout department. Choose a graphic that illustrates the benefit stated in your headline. For example, if your headline is "Travel Back in Time," a graphic showing a grandfather/grandson playing with a train set provides visual support for your main concept.

Make an Offer

Your ad should give readers a compelling reason to come into your store. The offer can be a special price on a particular class of items (sports memorabilia, for example), a giveaway (tickets, a drawing) or simply a coupon. Coupons are popular; readers will often read a coupon (even if they haven't read the ad) just to see what they can get.

Call to Action

You've given your ad a good headline, a supportive graphic and compelling body copy. Now, tell your customer what you want them to do: call for details, visit your website, come into the store, buy online, or something else. If you want your ad to deliver a response, you have to include a call to action. If you don't, then all you have provided is some entertaining reading material.

Let's use the information above to rewrite Joe's ad, step-by-step. Here are Joe's assumptions about his target group and the offer he has devised:

1. Joe has decided to create some new buyers for his art and home décor items. His shop is in northern Virginia, which has a high median income and lots of people moving in, moving out, and moving up. His target group is upwardly mobile Gen-Y 30-something women.

2. Joe has some good testimonials, so he will use one for his headline hook.

3. Joe's offer: Joe has an abundance of open edition art prints that he bought for a good price at auction. He'll offer a 2-for-1 coupon for these prints.

Here's how Joe's ad might read (the image used in the ad is a photo of Joe's store showing the variety of his inventory):

"No One Else Has A Lamp Like Mine!"
Sue Customer
Fairfax, VA

Express yourself with unique decorative items from Joe's *Wall Décor *Lamps *Occasional tables *Glass & porcelain
This Weekend Only! 2-4-1 Art Prints
While supplies last! Visit our website for coupon!
Joe's Antiques 123 Main St. Arlington VA 703-555-5555 Come in or visit us online at: www.joesantiques.com
Open 7 Days 10-6

Uniqueness is an important characteristic of Gen Y, hence the headline appealing to that trait. Cookie cutter decorating from a catalog is out of favor with Gen Y women, so the appeal to personal uniqueness is repeated in the sub-heading. The 2-for-1 offer appeals to new homeowners who have a lot of empty wall space to cover, and the photo supports Joe's claim to have a large variety of items. The coupon is good for only one weekend, which motivates the reader to go into the store right away. Making the coupon available online will drive traffic to Joe's website.

There are dozens of ways that this ad can be repurposed, depending on the merchandise that Joe wants to sell. The basic principles, however, remain the same.

Tap the Probate System to Win the Competition for Great Antiques

I t's no secret that antique dealers spend as much (or more) time acquiring inventory than they do selling it. Many dealers are up at the crack of dawn on weekends and spend their days searching estate sales, auctions, flea markets and antiques shows for merchandise. Some dealers take out-of-state road trips, and a few travel abroad to find inventory.

Others systematically work the online auction sites like eBay to find bargain treasures for re-sale. Almost all have spent years developing a network of pickers who can keep new inventory rolling in. Compared to antiques dealers, retailers of consumer goods have it easy. All they have to do to keep their shelves stocked is pick up the phone or go online and place a wholesale order from a catalog.

The reason that dealers are such early birds when mining estate sales, flea markets and antique shows is obvious: They want to find the best merchandise and negotiate a good price before their competitors show up. Flea market and estate sale sellers sometimes don't know what their merchandise is worth, and may accept an early cash offer.

Once "the competition" shows up and starts expressing interest in the same items, even an uninformed seller will hold the line on — or even raise — prices. In the antiques trade, where cost prices are negotiable and markups can be considerable, finding just a few special items a month can mean the difference between a meager profit and an outstanding profit.

So, if being first is good and less competition is good, it stands to reason that the best strategy for finding great deals is to jump to the head of the line and eliminate the competition altogether. Some dealers have already figured out this strategy, but not many. It's called working courthouse probate records.

For those unfamiliar with courthouse probate records, let's begin by understanding what probate is and end with a plan for mining probate records to find antiques and collectibles.

Probate is the process of proving the will of a deceased person. A decedent's debts must be paid and property distributed according to their wishes. In most states, this process is overseen by a Probate Court, but sometimes it's called an Orphan's Court. A probate court decides the legal validity of the will, grants approval to proceed with its execution and appoints an individual to execute the provisions of the will. This individual is called an executor or administrator.

In the antiques trade, finding just a few special items a month can mean the difference between a meager profit and an outstanding profit.

Generally, an executor is a friend or member of the decedent's family, but doesn't have to be. Sometimes the court appoints an executor, usually an attorney with experience in estate matters. It's the executor's job to pay all of the estate's debts, distribute property and file the tax returns. In return for these efforts, an executor is compensated. The amount of compensation is governed by state law.

Upon an individual's death, the will must be filed at the courthouse to begin the probate process. Once an estate has been opened for probate, there is a continuous stream of paperwork that must be submitted to the court by the executor. Such paperwork becomes part of the probate records.

The filing that is of most interest to antiques dealers is the estate inventory, which lists all of the assets of the estate — both titled property (autos, boats, real estate) and nontitled property (artwork, jewelry, cash, collectibles, antiques).

Typically, inventories must be filed within 45 days of the date of death. Probate records are a matter of public record; anyone can view them. Antiques dealers can have full access to a list of the estate's collectibles and know what's coming to market months ahead of anyone else, simply by researching courthouse probate records.

What you'll learn from looking at probate records:

1. The names and addresses of the executors and heirs and the location of the assets.

2. If the estate is likely to have cash flow problems. You'll learn how much cash is on hand to pay bills and if there are securities that can easily be liquidated to raise cash.

3. If there are antiques and collectibles available that might be for sale. You'll also learn which heirs will be inheriting which antiques, and their addresses. Don't be concerned if an item of interest is already assigned; you never know how an heir will respond to an inheritance. If the decedent's niece decorates her home in Zuo Modern, it's unlikely that she'll be interested in a living room full of Victorian furniture. There's nothing she'd like better than a cash offer from an antiques dealer.

The weaknesses in the probate system that can be pursued by antiques dealers:

1. Often, there is not enough cash in the estate to pay ongoing expenses and settle debts. If there is a home, mortgages and utilities must be paid, grass has to be cut and the home maintained until it can be sold. When an estate is heavy on assets and short on cash, smaller assets (like collections) will sometimes be liquidated to pay bills until the larger assets (like the home) can be dealt with.

2. Being an executor can be an overwhelming job, and virtually all executors need help to get the job done. Most executors are not professionals, and they don't have a clue what the household items and collectibles are worth or how to get an estate inventory done.

3. Families are busier and becoming more spread out. On top of the 15-20 hours per week that executors spend closing out an estate, they have jobs, families, and personal commitments. Sometimes, they live out-of-state (although courts can choose to appoint an in-state executor).

In short, most executors are overworked and short on cash. Anything you can do to make their job easier is usually appreciated.

Here's a three-step plan to mine probate records to find antique inventory:

1. Become familiar with the records department of your county District Court. This is where the probate records are generally kept. Probate filings are listed in the public records notices of your local newspaper; that's where you will find the names of the decedents. County Clerks are there to help the public gain access to the records, and most are very friendly. If you live in a large metropolitan area, it's likely that your courthouse records are available online. Sometimes online access is free; sometimes it isn't. Whether you search records in person or online doesn't matter; you'll find the same information.

2. Understand your competition. Few auctioneers, antiques dealers and estate sale companies work probate records. Such companies tend to be reactive (wait for someone to call them) rather than proactive (search probate records). However, there are companies who are not in the antiques business that actively pursue estate executors; they are called probate liquidators. Learn who the probate liquidators are in your city and what services they offer.

3. Develop a systematic approach for contacting executors and heirs. I won't suggest a system, because you have to be comfortable enough with whatever you devise to be willing to apply it regularly. Hit-and-miss marketing delivers hit-and-miss results. If all you can do is a monthly postcard mailing, then that's what you should do, but do it every month.

You've heard of lawyers who are ambulance chasers? Don't become a hearse-chaser; it will negatively affect your reputation. Unless you plan to offer executors your help to do the estate inventory, wait for the inventory to be filed before you make contact with anyone. When you do make contact, be sensitive to the fact that a loved one has recently passed away.

Dealers who conscientiously pursue probate records (especially those who are fortunate enough to have online courthouse access) will find that they spend less windshield time acquiring new inventory. And, their competitors will wonder how they keep getting the best deals.

An Antique Shop Owner's Exit Strategy Takes Time and Preparation

If the Grim Reaper had to earn a living like the rest of us, he'd probably become an auctioneer. He would trade his hood for a snappy-looking hat and his scythe for a gavel. He would preside over the demise of businesses, and as each asset passed the block his gavel would sound like thunder as he proclaimed "Sold!" in a voice that echoed with finality. The business owners would look on helplessly, stunned by the speed at which their life's work evaporated.

Some businesses will be out of reach of the Reaper. According to a 2008 White House Advisors Survey, about 12 percent of all closely held business owners have a written plan to sell their business intact and continue operations. Those business owners will cash out in style, selling at the right time to the right buyer for the right price. The remaining businesses will be sold piecemeal and shut down.

Most of the 40,000+ antiques businesses in the United States choose the auction option when the owners decide to close. Few of the antiques dealers I have spoken with are actually prepared for their inevitable exit. Overwhelmingly, dealers agree on the importance of an exit strategy, but few have done anything about it. Most dealers are uncertain about how to plan an exit strategy. Uncertainty leads to procrastination, and procrastination eventually leads to auction day.

Planning for the intact sale of an antiques business comes with its own special challenges. *The 2008 Business Reference Guide* quotes a "leading expert" as saying of the antiques business: "There are no rules of thumb for this type of business" and "handling inventory can be a real problem." In spite of the "leading expert's" statement that there are no hard and fast rules for selling an antiques store, the guide offers at least one rule of thumb: Price the business at 20 percent of annual sales plus the value of the inventory.

Pricing an antiques store as quoted above is hardly to the advantage of the seller. Most business brokers charge a commission of 10 percent of the gross selling price, and it is not unusual to have another 10 percent of the selling price eaten up by attorney and CPA fees. Deduct fees and commissions, and the dealer is left with less than the value of the inventory. When the value of the business comes down to just the inventory (let's skip the lawyers and brokers), call the auctioneer directly.

The time it takes to prepare a business to sell at auction can be calculated in months. The time it takes to prepare a business to sell via private sale is calculated in years. An owner liquidating through auction is paid only for the hard assets sold. An owner selling a "going concern" is paid the value of the hard assets, plus the combined values of the employee team, customer list, reputation of the business, and present value of future profits.

Consequently, some antiques dealers don't want to liquidate and walk away; they will lose money. Their business creates regular profits, has good cash flow, a nice facility and inventory, and a good staff. How does such a dealer move into the 12 percent of businesses that are sold intact and continue operations? What do these dealers need to do in order to sell at the right time to the right buyer for the right price?

Peter Drucker is quoted as saying, "The best way to predict the future is to create it." So, let's create a future wherein you are one of the dealers that sells when you are ready, for the best price, to the best buyer.

Sell only when you are ready

When it comes to selling your business as a going concern you have to be prepared to prove everything and supply a lot of financial details. Having a written business plan that can be used for comparison to your financial statements will be beneficial, as well as an operations manual (job descriptions, relationships, and suppliers). If your records are not particularly well kept, it will take three to five years to get your business ready to sell, plus a few years to find a buyer. You will need to keep your books and accounts scrupulously for several years and assemble your operating documents.

If you have your accounting and tax records in good order for the past three to five years, you are ready to assemble your advisory team and may begin to market your business when your exit plan is completed. In most cases, you can expect to have your business sold within two to three years. When I say "good order," I mean income statements, balance sheets, cash flow statements, inventory and asset schedules, and up-to-date tax schedules.

Sell at the right price

As discussed, finding the right price for an antiques store can be difficult. The "book value" of the business on your financial statements seldom comes close to accurately representing the worth of your business. Also, terms affect price. If you are willing to carry back a secured note for all or part of the selling price, you will sell your business faster and get a higher price.

Understand that all the legitimate tax-reducing techniques you have used over the years have had the cumulative effect of lowering the value of your business. Your income statement should be recast to add back to profits all non-cash and discretionary expenses that you have deducted over the years. Interest, depreciation, your pickup truck, cell phone, and anything else that the business pays for at your discretion should be added back into your profits.

Overwhelmingly, dealers agree on the importance of an exit strategy, but few have done anything about it.

Your accountant best handles the recasting of your income statement, but there are software programs available for less than $100 that can give you a quick value snapshot. I use software called BizPricer, but there are dozens of others available. Just Google "business valuation software."

Sell to the right buyer

Dealing in antiques is a lifestyle business. Antiques dealers are predominantly collectors who are passionate about their subject and have years of insider knowledge and experience. Such individuals make up a small percentage of the general population, and an even smaller percentage of entrepreneurs searching for a business to buy. The best prospects to purchase an antiques store are dealers who are looking to expand into other markets, serious collectors who are looking to turn their hobby into their profession, and restorers who want to add a retail operation to their restoration business.

Begin with the end in mind

In his book, *The Seven Habits of Highly Effective People*, Stephen R. Covey lists the second habit as "begin with the end in mind." Antiques dealers who plan ahead for their inevitable exit from business will find that over the years they are building wealth, not just income. And their business will become one of the few that avoids the Reaper's auction gavel.

Antiques Inheritances Affected By 2013 Gift Tax Changes

Word on the street is that collectibles appraisers have had a busy year. With the lifetime gift tax exemption scheduled to drop from $5 million to $1 million on Jan. 1, 2013, collectors are scuffling to pass on as much tax-free wealth as possible to their children and heirs.

Collectors who gift this year will save themselves some money in gift taxes, as well, because the gift tax rate jumps from 35 percent to 55 percent on the same date. The individual who gives the gift pays the taxes on any amounts over their lifetime gifting exemption at the rate current at the time of the gift. So, even if you're approaching your lifetime gifting limit, if you are sitting on a valuable collection that will someday pass to an heir, now is the time to consider how you will transfer the property.

As the filing deadline closes in, both collectors and appraisers will be pressured to get appraisals and paperwork done on time. Mistakes will be made. In a rush, collectors will turn to "quick and dirty" appraisal methods that will be rejected by the IRS and they will end up paying additional money in taxes, fines, and penalties. The appraisers who performed the valuations for the rejected tax returns may be heavily fined and barred for life from submitting appraisals to the IRS. When it comes to gifting collections, both collectors and appraisers need to move cautiously.

Collectors who don't plan to gift any of their collection this year may also be interested in this discussion, because at some point in the future, their collection will pass to someone else, whether by gift, bequest, or sale. It's been estimated that in the next 40 years, billions of dollars of wealth in the form of collectibles, will pass to succeeding generations.

The IRS looks at the valuations of comic books, musical instruments, coins, art, and other collectibles closely. My intent is to raise a few "red flags" for collectors who may be moving forward with gifting all or part of a collection this year. My usual disclaimer applies: I am not an accountant or attorney and cannot legally give tax advice. I can't even spell IRS. But I have performed gift appraisals and have never had one of my appraisals questioned by Uncle Sam.

My role is like that of a driving instructor: I can tell you where the hazards in the road are, but I'm not the traffic cop. You have to do your own driving. If you plan on gifting, seek professional tax advice.

The 2013 deadline aside, there are other issues to be considered when gifting a collection. For example, what amount will be taxed? Gifted collections keep the tax basis/value they had when they were gifted, but inherited collections assumed fair market value at the time they were inherited. What will the tax rate be? Will the tax be paid on ordinary income (if the collection was part of a business operation) or as investment income? There may not be much difference between the two rates; investment collections are taxed at 28 percent, not the 15 percent that most people assume. Add in the possibility of tax claw-back, future income taxes, and IRA complications,

Even if you're approaching your lifetime gifting limit, now is the time to consider how you will transfer the property.

and you can see why you need to consult with a tax expert. Makes my head spin just to read this paragraph. Here's how this may translate in the real world:

My client, Doug, had been downsized and needed to raise some cash while he looked for a job. Twenty-five years ago, Doug had removed a guitar collection from his wealthy father's estate before the inventory was taken, so the guitars were not included in the estate. Doug reasoned that his father had always intended for him to have the guitars but had never gotten around to saying so in his will. My job was to appraise the guitars and recommend selling options for the instruments. After some research, I told Doug that the guitars had a combined value just over six figures. He was also surprised to learn that he might have both a criminal problem and a tax problem today because of his action 25 years ago.

Establishing the value of the guitars 25 years ago with any certainty would be difficult today, but it is certain that they had appreciated from their original cost (the original tax basis). Had they been included in the estate inventory, their tax basis when Doug acquired them would have been established (fair market value), but no appraiser ever saw the guitars. Since Doug's father had a large estate, the guitars would undoubtedly have been subject to estate tax. The guitars were not included in the estate inventory, so the tax on them was never paid.

If Doug sells the guitars, he will make a handsome profit, and he will owe capital gains taxes (at the 28 percent rate for collectibles). If the IRS decides to audit the return, they will certainly want Doug to provide purchase receipts to establish the tax basis for the guitars. If it is discovered that Doug removed the guitars from his father's estate, Doug will owe the unpaid estate taxes plus penalties and interest, and may face criminal fraud charges (there is no statute of limitations on fraud).

The lesson? If you intend for your heirs to inherit your collection, you will save everyone a lot of money and trouble by gifting the collection while you are still alive. The other lesson? Don't think you can con the IRS. They will find you, and then fine you.

Perhaps the most important consideration in gifting is the value placed on your collection. Unless you have purchase receipts to validate the original cost of each item, you will need to have your collection appraised. "Appraisal" is one of those words that are so casually tossed around that it is almost meaningless. We regularly see "Appraisal Fairs" offered by dealers and appraisers alike. Make no mistake: What you are getting at such events is not an appraisal; it is an unsubstantiated personal opinion. Of course, we all know that home appraisals have strict rules and a specific format. Most folks are unaware that the IRS requires personal property appraisals to follow the same rules and be submitted in a similar format. If you've had your local auctioneer or antique/collectibles dealer make a list of your items and assign them a value, this list is not an appraisal that the IRS will accept. Neither will the IRS accept an online appraisal given from a photograph.

If you are going to have your collection appraised, make sure that your appraiser has successfully submitted appraisals to the IRS for the type of collection that you will be gifting. If you can't find such a person, here's what the IRS expects:

Unquestioned expertise proven through either education or experience (certification or training from an appraisal organization or verifiable industry training and/or experience).

Follow the format prescribed by the Uniform Standards of Professional Appraisal Practice (USPAP).

Whether you plan to gift your collection this year or in 10 years, most folks find that gifting is a better solution for their family than bequeathing a collection through a will. Either way, proceed with caution.

19th - Mid 20th Century:

Baccarat
Belleek - Irish
Buffalo Pottery
Carnival Glass
Doulton - Royal Doulton
Ironstone China
Limoges
Majolica
Mary Gregory
Royal Dux
Royal Worcester
Satin Glass
Staffordshire
Wedgwood
Zsolnay
&
American Antiques

Antique Legacies